Rebels on the Red

Confederates of the Red River Campaign

From
Avoyelles to Mansfield
and back

150th Anniversary Edition

Compiled from field reports and letters

Illustrated by period newspaper and modern images along with portraits in uniform of some of the Confederate soldiers of the Red River Campaign.

Randy DeCuir
www.thelouisianapurchase.net

The Battle of Mansfield was fought on April 8, 1864, just south of the town of Mansfield, Louisiana. The battle was part of the Red River Campaign, a Union effort to wrest control of the Red River and capture the City of Shreveport. Shreveport was the Confederate capital of Louisiana, a busy river port with an active cotton economy, the site of military industry, including ship and submarine construction, and the head of the Texas Trail. The capture of Shreveport would have allowed Union forces to enter Texas and crush the supplies moving from Texas, Mexico and western points to supply Confederate forces in the east.

The Battle of Mansfield saw the defeat of Union forces under the command of General Nathaniel Banks by Confederate forces commanded by General Richard Taylor. It was the last major Confederate victory of the Civil War.

This volume attempts to put a face to the Conderate names of this historic chapter of the Civil War.

**Please email additions and corrections please to:
decuir@yahoo.com**

Cover Photo: Grand Encore in Natchitoches Parish during the Red River Campaign

Sources include but not limited to:
William J. Bozic, Jr., Steve Mayeux, Carlos Mayeux, Jr., Dr. Sue Lyles Eakin, Wayne Cosby, Official Records of the War of Rebellion, National Park Service.

Table of Contents

Section I
History of the Red River Campaign

Section II
Portraits of Confederates in uniform who served during the Red River Campaign

Section III
Confederate Order of Battle

REBEL ATTACK ON GUN-BOATS IN THE RED RIVER
- from Harper's Illustrated Weekly, May 14, 1864

Section I
History of the Red River Campaign

The Red River Campaign
Spring, 1864

AVOYELLES PARISH
March 11 – Yankees cross **Atchafalaya** at Simmesport
March 13 - **Boute de Bayou** skirmish near Moreauville
March 14 – Confederate **Fort DeRussy** is captured

RAPIDES PARISH
March 16-20 –Union troops occupy **Alexandria**
March 21 – Skirmish at **Henderson Hill**

NATCHITOCHES PARISH
March 31 – Union troops occupy **Natchitoches**
April 2 – Skirmish at **Crump's Corner**
April 3 – Union captures Port of **Grand Ecore**

DESOTO PARISH
April 7 – Skirmishes at **Wilson's Farm & Tenmile Bayou**
April 8 – Battle of **Sabine Crossroads (Mansfield)**

SABINE PARISH
April 9 – Battle of **Pleasant Hill**

NATCHITOCHES PARISH
April 10-21 -Union troops hold up at **Grand Ecore**
April 23 - Battle of **Cloutierville & Monette's Ferry**

RAPIDES PARISH
May 1 – Entire Union army back in **Alexandria**
May 4 - Union positioned north of Gov. Moore's Plantation
May 7 – Union navy retires to **Alexandria**
May 8 - Chamber's Plantation engagement (LSU-A Site)
May 11 -13 Bailey's Dam built to free trapped ships

AVOYELLES PARISH
May 4 - USS Covington & Warner sink at **Dunn's Bayou**
May 16 - **Battle of Marksville**
May 17 – Battle of **Mansura**
May 18– Battle of **Moreauville**
May 18 – Battle of **Yellow Bayou**
May 19- Union crosses **Atchafalaya**, to **Baton Rouge**

January, 1864...
...Yankees Prepare to invade Red River

Report of U.S. Major General Nathaniel Banks

The defenses of the enemy consisted of a series of works covering the approaches to Galveston and Houston from the south, the defenses of Galveston Bay, Sabine Pass, and Sabine River, Fort De Russy, a formidable work located 3 miles from Marksville for the defense of the Red River, and extensive and formidable works at Trinity, the junction of the Tensas and Washita at Camden, commanding approaches from the north.

To meet these forces of the enemy it was proposed to concentrate, in some general plan of operations, 15,000 of the troops under command of General Steele, a detachment of 10,000 from the command of General Sherman, and a force from 15,000 to 17,000 men from the Army of the Gulf, making an army of 35,000 to 37,000 men of all arms, with such gun-boats as the Navy Department should order. Orders were given to my command at once to suspend operations at Galveston, and vigorous preparations were made for the new campaign.

...The organization of the troops of my command assigned to the expedition was intrusted to Maj. Gen. W. B. Franklin. The main body of his command, consisting of the Nineteenth Corps (except Grover's division at Madisonville, which was to join him) and one division of the Thirteenth Corps, under General Ransom, were at this time on Berwick Bay, between Berwick City and Franklin, on the Bayou Teche, directly on the line of march for Alexandria and Shreveport. Small garrisons were left at Brownsville and Matagorda Bay in Texas positions which, under instructions from the President and subsequently from Lieutenant-General Grant, were not to be abandoned), at New Orleans, and at Port Hudson, which was threatened by a vigorous and active enemy; smaller garrisons at Baton Rouge and Donaldsonville, on the river, and at Pensacola and Key West, on the coast, constituted the balance of forces under my command.

February, 1864...Jefferson Davis

Jefferson Davis wrote about the Red River campaign in his book *The Rise and Fall of the Confederacy* he authored after the war:

In the Red River country of Louisiana it became certain in February, 1864, that the enemy was about to make an expedition against our forces under General Richard Taylor, not so much to get possession of the country as to obtain the cotton in that region. Their forces were to be commanded by Major General Banks, and to consist of his command, augmented by a part of Major General Sherman's army from Vicksburg, and accompanied by a fleet of gunboats under Admiral Porter. With these the force under General Steele, in Arkansas, was to Cooperate. Taylor's forces at this time consisted of Harrison's mounted regiment with a four-gun battery, in the north toward Monroe; Mouton's brigade, near Alexandria; Polignac's, at Trinity, on the Washita, fiftyfive miles distant; Walker's division, at Marksville and toward Simmsport, with two hundred men detached to assist the gunners at Fort De Russy, which, though still unfinished, contained eight heavy guns and two field pieces. Three companies of mounted men were watching the Mississippi, and the remainder of a regiment was on the Teche.

Jefferson Davis

March 10, 1864...Depart Vicksburg

Report of U.S. General A. J. Smith

    The troops under my command, consisting of five regiments of infantry of the First Division, Sixteenth Army Corps, under the immediate command of Brig. Gen. Joseph A. Mower, ten regiments of infantry and two batteries of light artillery of the Third Division, Sixteenth Army Corps (my own division), and six regiments of infantry and one battery of light artillery from the Seventeenth Army Corps, under the command of Brig. Gen. Thomas Kirby Smith, left Vicksburg at 6 p.m. on the 10th day of March, 1864, on transports, pursuant to orders from you, which were in effect as follows:

    To proceed with the command to the mouth of the Red River, where I would find Admiral Porter with a portion of the Mississippi Squadron to convoy my fleet up Red River, and after conference with him to proceed to Alexandria, La., and report to Maj. Gen. N. P. Banks, commanding Department of the Gulf, reaching Alexandria, if possible, on the 17th of March, from which point Major-General Banks would assume the command and direction of the expedition in person.

U. S. Major Gen. Nathaniel Banks   U. S. Admiral David Porter

Diary of Sgt. Charles Ewringmann of 27th Iowa US Infantry:
On the 10th of March we left Vicksburg with a fleet of around 20 transports, passed Natchez and Port Adams on the 11th and arrived shortly at the mouth of the Red River where we anchored for the night.

Porter's fleet on Red River during the war from period images

March, 1864...Simmesport

History of Fort at Simmesport
by Steve Mayeux, Historian, Simmesport Historical Society

Building of Fort Humbug at Yellow Bayou:
This Civil War fort was established by Gen. Dick Taylor to protect the Atchafalaya River and other tributaries from the Union forces. It was named "Old Oaks" by the Union forces, "Norwood Plantation Fort" by the local people and "Fort Humbug" by the soldiers who used it. Historians later named the site "Yellow Bayou Civil War Fort"

Fort Humbug was a complex of forts and earthworks constructed at the junction of Yellow Bayou and Bayou des Glaises, near the village of Simmesport in Avoyelles Parish, Louisiana, for the purpose of preventing the movement of Union troops into central Louisiana. Its construction began shortly before December 15, 1863, by Scurry's Brigade of Walker's Texas Division, confederate states Army, and construction continued on the works until March 3, 1864. Fort Humbug was abandoned by Confederate forces on March 12, 1864, and was destroyed by Union engineers in late May of the same year. Only a small portion of the original Fort Humbug remains in existence, and can be seen on the south side of La. Highway 1, just west of Simmesport.

The fortifications at Fort Humbug were on the west bank of Yellow Bayou and on both banks of Bayou des Glaises, and consisted of "extensive works extending for near two miles in length," and included "forts, glacis, rifle pits etc etc. The four regiments of Scurry's Brigade were camped from one to three miles up Bayou des Glaise, housed in abandoned slave quarters on the Norwood plantation, and worked on the fortifications on a rotating schedule, one regiment working every forth day, seven days a week. (It was noticed, however, that "the boys don't work well on Sunday. They don't have the vim that they would on another day.") Working by reliefs, the individual soldiers would work for one hour and rest for one hour. The cold weather and

March, 1864...Simmesport

frequent rains (including at least one snowfall) made for miserable working conditions, but in general the soldiers working on the fort were "living tolerable well." They had plenty of corn bread and poor beef, as well as sugar and molasses, with occasional pork, potatoes, and flour.

The "Humbug"

The name Fort Humbug would appear to have been unofficial, and probably stemmed from the average soldier's belief that the fort was, in fact, totally useless. In a letter to his wife dated December 20, writing from "Camp on Bayou des Glaises," six miles from Simmesport, Dr. Edward Cade of Walker's Division stated "Our command is engaged in throwing up quite an extensive line of earth works, though I think it labor thrown away as they are perfectly useless." Captain Elijah Petty, of Company F, 17th Texas Volunteer Infantry, Scurry's Brigade, explained the situation in a letter home to his wife in mid-January: "This is one of the routes by which it can be flanked. But there are 3 other routes by which is as good or better than this and why this alone is defined is more than I can tell. The other routes that I refer to are 1st By the way of Barracks Bay, New Iberia etc the way that Genl. Banks approached Alexandria last spring, 2nd By the way of Morgan's ferry up Bayou Rouge by Cheneyville etc, and #rd and best route is up Red River, up Black River,up Little River through Catahoula Lake and by water to within 18 miles of Alexandria. If we had a force and works to guard all these routes I could see some practicability in the work that we are doing here. Otherwise it appears nonsensical."

Another problem which existed with the defense of Fort Humbug was the fact that it's southern flank was defended solely by a usually impassive swamp, which would be dry and quite passable in March of 1864, leaving the fort completely suseptible to encirclement.

Not everyone felt that Fort Humbug was a fraud, however. One Confederate staff officer, Felix Pierre Poche, castigated General Scurry for abandoning the fort, feeling that the

March, 1864...Simmesport

Texans should have been able to hold the position in spite of being outnumbered twelve to one! In a March 13, 1864 diary entry, Poche stated "I learned that Genl. Scurry in needless fright had foolishly retreated before the enemy, abandoning his well constructed and formidable camp on Yellow Bayou in the night on Saturday."

Union Knowledge of Fort Humbug

Union forces had been made aware of the construction of Fort Humbug by early January, 1864. On January 7, Charles C. Dwight, Commanding Officer of the 160th New York Volunteers, reported receiving word from Lt. Commander Frank M. Ramsey, commander of the gunboat squadron at the mouth of Red River, that "the enemy is fortifying at the junction of Bayou Yellow and Bayou des Glaize, about 1 mile west of the Atchafalaya. In a report dated January 8, Lt. Commander Ramsay officially reported learning from a refugee that "A small fortification has been built back of Simmesport at the junction of Yellow Bayou with Bayou des Glaises, and there is breastwork, with a couple of fieldpieces, about half a mile below Simmesport, on the Atchafalaya."

By January 12, Ramsay had picked up "several deserters and refugees" and noted that "They also confirm the report about the fortification at the junction of Yellow Bayou and Bayou des Glaises. Scurry's brigade is stationed there. He has only field guns. More confirmations followed. On January 23, Brigadier General George L. Andrews (Commanding, Port Hudson), reported "Two negroes just in from Grosstete report 600 of Walker's command were at the place on Wednesday last conscripting colored men, mules, and oxen, to be used on fortifications at Simsport, which place the rebels are reported to be fortifying." On January 28, Brigadier general Daniel Ullman, also at Port Hudson, reported that four deserters, one refugee and one prisoner had been brought in, and had provided information "that General Walker has erected a large and strong work at the junction of Yellow Bayou and Bayou des Glaize."

March, 1864...Simmesport

The "Grand Skedaddle"

    General A. J. Smith of the United States Army arrived at Simmesport on March 12, 1864, with approximatley 18,000 men (21 regiment infantry, 3 batteries of light artillery, and elements of the Mississippi Marine Brigade). First indications were that the landing would be made with about 2,000 men, and Scurry's Brigade made preparations to defend against this attack. When the true scope of the invasion was discovered, Fort Humbug was abandoned and the "Grand Skedaddle" was on, not to end until April 8, near Mansfield where the "skeddadle" would reverse, and turn into one of the last great Confederate victories of the War. Meanwhile, Scurry's Brigade moved to near Moreauville, where it linked up with the rest of Walker's Division. Wagons were sent back to the old camp site for tents and other baggage, but this resulted in the capture of several wagons and drivers, and the tents were lost anyway. As the Union column moved past Fort Humbug on the morning of March 13th, they found "the camp broken up and the enemy gone; the bridge leading across the stream burning, and evidence of fright. There are two extensive earthworks, still incomplete, and a prodigious raft being constructed across Bayou Glaize so as to prevent the gunboats ascending the little channel during high-water." A soldier of the 8th Wisconsin Infantry referred to the fort at this time as Fort Scurry, and cleverly announced that "the garrison did not wait for an attack and taking the name of their fort for their motto 'scurried' away across the country to a place of safety..."

    The abandonment of Fort Humbug marked the opening of the Red River Campaign. Two months later the fort would be involved again in the final days of the campaign.

March 11, 1864...Simmesport

Report of U.S. General A. J. Smith

On arriving at the mouth of the Red River, at about 12 m., March 11, 1864, a dispatch was received from Major-General Banks, stating that the heavy rains had so delayed his column that he would not be able to reach Alexandria before March 21, 1864. On conferring with Admiral Porter, I learned that Fort DeRussy, a strong fort on the right bank of Red River, equidistant from the mouth of Red River and Alexandria, and mounting ten guns, had been garrisoned by the enemy and which it would be necessary to take before we could proceed to Alexandria. It was therefore deemed best to act against it in conjunction, the army in the rear by land and the navy by river. Leaving the mouth of Red River at about 12 m., March 12, 1864, we proceeded up Red River to the mouth of the Atchafalaya Bayou; thence with the transports down the Atchafalaya Bayou to Simmesport, a point on its right bank near the mouth of Bayou De Glaize and 30 miles by land from Fort DeRussy, reaching Simmesport at about 5 p.m. of the same day.

Troop movement seen at Simmesport during the Civil War. Atchafalaya River in background.

March 12, 1864...Bayou des Glaises

Report of Major General John G. Walker, CSA

Yellow Bayou, 4 miles from Simmesport....the enemy had landed a small force that day at the latter point. Enemy's force was very large, occupying twenty-seven transports and escorted by fourteen gun-boats, and that they were then debarking at Simmesport with their artillery and (wagon) trains.

The night of the 12th... General Scurry's fell back to the west of Bayou De Glaize and took position at the long bridge at Bout De Bayou, to resist the enemy's advance. Walker left Red River towards Bayou des Glaises.

Report of Major General John G. Walker, CSA to Major E. Surget:

I have the honor to report, for the information of the major-general commanding the District of West Louisiana, that on the 12th instant I was informed by Brigadier-General Scurry, commanding on Yellow Bayou, 4 miles from Simmesport, that the enemy had landed a small force that day at the latter point. I received this information at 5 p.m., which I immediately dispatched to you. At 7 p.m. of the same day I dispatched to you the subsequently received intelligence from General Scurry that the enemy's force was very large, occupying twenty-seven transports and escorted by fourteen gun-boats, and that they were then debarking at Simmesport with their artillery and trains.

Upon the first information General Scurry had moved down in the direction of the Atchafalaya with the purpose of attacking the enemy and driving him aboard of his vessels, but subsequent and more correct information as to the strength of the enemy induced him to fall back to Moreauville, 11 miles west of Simmesport. The defenses constructed with so much labor at Yellow Bayou were rendered useless by the drying up of the swamps on the

March 12, 1864...Bayou des Glaises

flanks, which were depended on as the chief means of defense. To avoid being cut off from Marksville by the enemy coming by a practicable road from Old River to the big bend of the De Glaize, this movement to the rear became necessary.

The night of the 12th was spent in withdrawing my infantry and light artillery from a point on Red River 7 or 8 miles below Fort De Russy and making preparations to march to General Scurry's support, who was instructed to delay the march of the enemy as much as possible, and in case he was pressed to fall back to the west of Bayou De Glaize and take position at the long bridge at Bout De Bayou, to resist the enemy's advance until I could re-enforce him.

Gen. Walker and Gen. Scurry of Texas

March 13, 1864...Boute De Bayou

Report of Major General John G. Walker, CSA

Walker reaches Bout De Bayou the next morning. I found that General Scurry had fallen back across the De Glaize and was taking position at the long bridge.... All the cavalry under my command having been cut off in Pointe Coupée by the entrance into the Atchafalaya of the enemy's gun-boats. I was wholly without the means of gaining information, as the enemy kept his front well covered by his small cavalry force. Late that night I received intelligence from Lieutenant Robinson, whom I had sent out to gain information, that from citizens he had learned that the enemy were re-embarking for the purpose of ascending Red River.

Report of Major General Walker, CSA to Major E. Surget:

Upon reaching Bout De Bayou the next morning I found that General Scurry had fallen back across the De Glaize and was taking position at the long bridge already mentioned. All the cavalry under my command having been cut off in Pointe Coupée by the entrance into the Atchafalaya of the enemy's gun-boats. I was wholly without the means of gaining information, as the enemy kept his front well covered by his small cavalry force. Late that night I received intelligence from Lieutenant Robinson, whom I had sent out to gain information, that from citizens he had learned that the enemy were re-embarking for the purpose of ascending Red River.

Report of U.S. General A. J. Smith

On the morning of the 13th, I sent out the two divisions of the Sixteenth Army Corps, under command of Brig. Gen. J. A. Mower, with directions to move out about 5 miles on the Fort De Russy road, capture or disperse any parties of the enemy in that vicinity, and gain all the information possible of the state of the roads and position of the enemy. The division of the Seventeenth Army Corps was ordered under arms to be in readiness to support him if necessary. About 3 miles from the landing, in the fork of the Yellow Bayou and Bayou De Glaize, General Mower came upon a brigade of the enemy, under command of General William R. Scurry,

March 13, 1864...Boute De Bayou

occupying a fort, then in process of construction, but who abandoned their work and fled at his approach. He pursued them about 2 miles, capturing 6 of their wagons and about 20 prisoners, when, having gained the necessary information and having no cavalry with which to make an effectual pursuit, I ordered him to return with his command to the landing. I immediately disembarked my land transportation, and, directing the transports to join the Mississippi Squadron under command of Admiral Porter and proceed with it to Fort DeRussy, moved forward my whole command on the road to Fort DeRussy. Leaving the landing at about 9 p.m., we bivouacked for the night 4 miles from Simmesport.

Report of U.S. Major General Nathaniel Banks
On the 13th of March, 1864, one division of the Sixteenth Corps, under Brigadier-General Mower, and one division of the Seventeenth Corps, under Brig. Gen. T. Kirby Smith, the whole under command of Brig. Gen. A. J. Smith, landed at Simsport, on the Atchafalaya, and proceeded at once toward Fort DeRussy, carrying it by assault at 4.30 p.m. on the afternoon of the 14th. Two hundred and sixty prisoners and 10 heavy guns were captured. Our loss was slight. The troops and transports, under General A. J. Smith, and the Marine Brigade, under General Ellet, with the gunboats, moved to Alexandria, which was occupied without opposition on the 16th of the same month. General Lee, of my command, arrived at Alexandria on the morning of the 19th. The enemy in the mean time continued his retreat through Cheneyville, in the direction of Shreveport.

History from National Park Service website:
Smith sent out some troops on the morning of the 13th to determine if any enemy was in their path. This force dispersed and chased an enemy brigade, after which, Smith set his men in motion up the Fort DeRussy road. They did not proceed far before night.

Union General A. J. Smith   *Confederate General Kirby Smith*

Hutton, King Art. at Fort DeRussy:

Capt. Hutton   Lt. Hervey   Capt. Barbin   J. B. Guillory

G. Fontenot   D. W. Madel   Hugh McNeal   A. J. Reed

March 14, 1864…Diary of the march

 Sgt. Charles Ewringmann, 27th Iowa US Infantry

While passing through Cocoville, between Mansura and Marksville, a Union officer posted guards at the Catholic Church while the troops marched through the area. He wanted to make sure the church was not ransacked or damaged. The church stood where the St. Paul Cemetery is located today.

The next afternoon we came through Mansura and in the evening to Marksville (beautiful prairie, nice church in the woods, many French) where we were placed as guards so that the army did not damage the church during our pass-through. While the first regiment was going through the town we heard shooting on the other side….

The Battle of Fort DeRussy, as illustrated in Frank Leslie's Weekly.

March 14...Fort DeRussy Falls

Report of U.S. General A. J. Smith to Maj. E. Surget:

Soon after daylight on the 14th, this information was proven incorrect by hearing the sound of numerous drums in the distance in the direction of Simsport, and as the morning advanced it became apparent that the enemy in force was approaching our position. As to his strength we could only form a conjecture, as he kept his front too well covered to permit our obtaining a view of his infantry column, until at about 8.30 o'clock in the morning it reached Moreauville, and turning to the left defiled along the banks of the De Glaize in full view of our pickets, whom they drove in by a musketry and artillery fire.

I commenced my movement to Bayou Du Lac bridge at 10 a.m. on the 14th, and not until the enemy, having repaired the burnt bridge over Bayou De Glaize, had commenced crossing his infantry in force. The road followed by my division diverges from the Marksville and Simsport road at Mansura.

The enemy, on reaching the intersection of the road on

March 14...Fort DeRussy Falls

which he was marching and that by which we were retiring, moved straight on to Fort De Russy without halting, his long column well closed up and leaving no stragglers behind. Moving slowly and halting frequently to watch the movements of the enemy, the rear of my column did not reach Bayou Du Lac until 4 p.m.

The enemy's column reached Marksville about 3 o'clock.... a column of about 4,000 men pushed directly through to Fort De Russy, while the greater portion of the command halted in the immediate vicinity of the village. Later I learned that the fort was invested about 4 p.m., and that a fierce musket and artillery fire was kept up until about sundown, when it ceased, and from the shout of the enemy it was supposed the fort then surrendered.

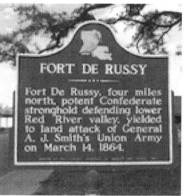

*Gen. DeRussy, builder of Fort DeRussy, at left.
Historic marker on Marksville courthouse square, at right*

Report of U.S. General A. J. Smith

At 3 o'clock on the morning of the 14th, I again moved forward toward Fort De Russy. Two bridges which we had to cross were set on fire by the retreating brigade of the

March 14...Fort DeRussy Falls

enemy, but were extinguished by our advance before they were seriously damaged. On reaching Mansura I learned that the bridges across the Bayou De Glaize had been destroyed, and that the rebel General Walker, commanding a division, had marched out from Fort De Russy with his command to the point where he supposed we would cross the bayou, about 5 miles west from Mansura, had formed a junction with Scurry's brigade, and intended to oppose our crossing. I immediately ordered the bayou to be bridged at Mansura, taking the material from an old cotton-gin, and by crossing companies at the same time on a ferry-boat had my whole command across before General Walker was aware that the advance had halted. Directing General Thomas Kirby Smith, who was at the rear of my column, to keep well closed up and watch carefully the left flank and rear, I at once moved forward toward Fort De Russy, leaving General Walker and his command on the left.

On arriving near the fort I found that it was occupied by a garrison of about 350 men. I therefore halted my column 1 miles from the fort, and, after covering my left flank and rear from any attack that Walker could possibly make, directed General Mower to advance with the First and Second Brigades of the Third Division, Sixteenth Army Corps, in line of battle, with skirmishers thrown well to the front, followed by the Third Brigade within supporting distance. As soon as the line came within sight of the fort the enemy opened upon it with five pieces of artillery from the fort, doing, however, but little execution. Their guns on the land side all being *en barbette*, the skirmishers of the Second Brigade soon silenced them.

At about 6.30 p.m. the order to charge was given, and the First and Second Brigades advanced under a scattering fire from the enemy, whose infantry were kept down by my skirmishers, and scaled the parapet within twenty minutes from the time the order to charge was given. The enemy then surrendered. Our loss was 3 killed and 35 wounded; total, 38.

March 14...Fort DeRussy Falls

Full lists of casualties and captures accompany this report. We captured 319 prisoners, 10 pieces of artillery, and a large quantity of ordnance and ordnance stores, marching during the day 26 miles, bridging a bayou, and capturing the fort before sunset. Among the pieces of artillery taken were two 9-inch Dahlgren guns, which were captured by the enemy, one from the steamer Indianola and one from the Harriet Lane. Owing to obstructions in the river the gun-boat fleet did not arrive until after the fort was captured. Of the artillery captured, four pieces were in the fort and six in a water battery on the bank of the river, about 400 yards from the fort, connected with it by a covered way. Two of the guns in the water battery were casemated, and the casemate plated with a double thickness of railroad iron. The fleet arrived during the night, and the gun-boats passed up the river. The artillery captured, with the exception of two 6-pounder iron guns, was taken on board the several boats of the fleet. All ordnance and ordnance stores captured have been taken up and accounted for by Lieut. J. B. Pannes, Seventeenth New York Infantry, acting ordnance officer.

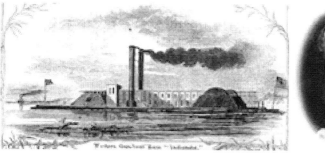

Indianola Steamship *John Ritland*

John (Jens) Ritland, Co. K, 32nd Iowa Infantry,, USA, wrote:
Now ensued the battle of Fort DeRussy, March 14, 1864. Cannons were brought into play, and we were fired upon as we marched along the road. Further on we were flanked aside on the banks of a creek where we dropped down flat on the ground. While lying thus, Colonel Scott shouted: "When the bugle is blown, you must all get up! Rise

March 14...Fort DeRussy Falls

as one man!" We lay quiet for about an hour, and when the summons came, we jumped to our feet and charged up the steep bluffs. I was nearly on the top once, but became so short of breath, that I hadn't the power to hold on, and slid back a considerable distance. I grabbed hold of an exposed root and pulled myself up again. In the meantime, the bullets flew thick and fast. Tom Lein said it was so steep where he happened to be that the men had to climb on each other's backs to be able to make headway. Our men swarmed in from all sides. I was of the first coming from the south side of the fort to reach the top, and we jumped in on the poor wretches as they stood or sat around, with the sweat just pouring off them from fear.

Report of Major General John G. Walker, CSA

Since reaching this camp two officers (Captain Adams, of the Twenty-eighth Texas Cavalry, dismounted, and Lieutenant Jennings, of the Thirteenth Texas Cavalry, dismounted), who formed a portion of the garrison at Fort De Russy, have come in, bringing in 21 men, with their arms and accouterments. They represent that the fort was attacked from the direction of Marksville about 4 p.m. on the 14th; that the enemy planted batteries at three or four points and soon rendered the water battery (where they were) untenable; that but one of the guns in the water battery could be trailed upon the enemy, and from which but one shot was fired, and that was from the 32-pounder rifle; that in consequence of the heavy artillery fire into the rear of the water battery they were forced into the excavations in front of the parapet, where they remained for some time, until it became apparent that they could do nothing and that in a few minutes they would be surrounded and captured. Under such circumstances Captain Adams, the ranking officer left (Captain Hutton, who had command of the work, having disappeared early in the action), concluded to withdraw the men and endeavor to make his escape. All came out, including Captain Hutton's own company, but they threw away their arms and one by

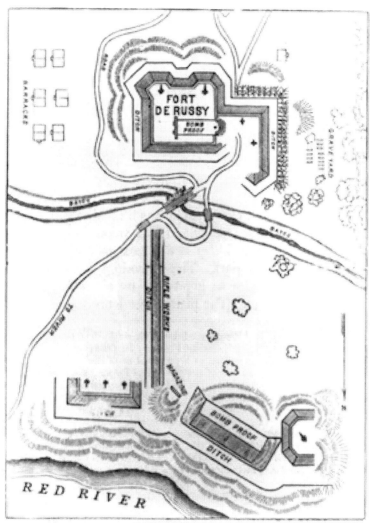

PLAN OF FORT DE RUSSY.

March 14...Fort DeRussy Falls

one disappeared, and, as Captain Adams supposes, returned to their homes. In striking contrast to this disgraceful conduct of Captain Hutton and his company, it is with great pleasure I record the gallant and noble conduct of a detachment of 9 men belonging to Captain King's company. Captain King, with the principal part of his company, was in the upper work, and this detachment, under Lieutenant Brooke, was sent to man one of the guns in the water battery. When it was proposed by the men here to make their escape, as they could do nothing, these 9 men declared their purpose of going into the upper fort to assist their comrades and share their fate, and amid a heavy fire of artillery and musketry set out with Lieutenant Brooke to carry out their design. Their fate is unknown, but such honorable and noble conduct deserves to be recorded.

I find upon examining the post returns of the fort, deducting those known to have escaped, that our loss does not exceed 205 enlisted men and 24 commissioned officers. The loss in material, especially in guns, is very heavy and perhaps irreparable. I succeeded, however, in saving two siege guns, a 24-pounder and a 30-pounder Parrott rifle, sent off early on the morning of the 14th. The only loss of material sustained by my division was 2 wagons and teams captured by the enemy from General Scurry's brigade while between Moreauville and Simsport.

In accounting for the disaster at Fort De Russy it is unnecessary to look to other causes than the overwhelming superiority of the enemy's force; but even with this disadvantage Fort De Russy might have been held for some days, perhaps, without relief from the outside, but for the vicious system of engineering adopted and the wretched judgment displayed in the selection of the position.

William Bringhurst, Captured at DeRussy

Confederates at Fort DeRussy:

8th Texas Infantry

Rev. J. Smith   Col. A. Hobby   1st Lt. Warren   Maj. Vernon

11th Texas Infantry

Pvt. W. Bates   Capt. Burton   John Busby.   W. Engledow

Henry Gill   F. M. Harris   Sam McDaniel   Col. Roberts

March 14...Fort DeRussy Falls
Report of Major General Walker, CSAm to Major E. Surget:

Soon after daylight on the 14th, this information was proven incorrect by hearing the sound of numerous drums in the distance in the direction of Simsport, and as the morning advanced it became apparent that the enemy in force was approaching our position. As to his strength we could only form a conjecture, as he kept his front too well covered to permit our obtaining a view of his infantry column, until at about 8.30 o'clock in the morning it reached Moreauville, and turning to the left defiled along the banks of the De Glaize in full view of our pickets, whom they drove in by a musketry and artillery fire. His column, then exposed to our view, extended for 2 miles along the banks of the De Glaize, through the village of Moreauville, and disappeared in the cut-off in the direction of the Atchafalaya. The force thus displayed consisted, as near as could be arrived at, of 15,000 to 17,000 infantry, thirty or forty pieces of light artillery, and a small cavalry force not exceeding 300. The enemy had no subsistence or baggage trains, and only his ordnance and hospital wagons.

In taking position at Bout De Bayou it had been my intention to give the enemy battle and hold him in check, at least until Mouton s brigade, which I supposed would reach me that night, could come up; but I soon found that the force of enemy was so overwhelming that my small division, numbering but 3,828 muskets present and twelve light guns, was entirely unequal to the task of checking more than momentarily the advance of the enemy. The position I had chosen offered some advantages against an enemy not so unequal in numbers, and if the swamps had been covered with water, as they usually are at this season of the year, even against a largely superior force; but the unusual dryness of the season had rendered the swampy grounds above and below Bout De Bayou bridge passable for artillery and trains, and rendered my position extremely hazardous, inasmuch as I was on [an] island formed by Red River, Bayous De Glaize, Du Lac, and Choctaw, the only outlet to which was Bayou Du Lac bridge, 8 miles to the south. In the event of the enemy turning my right, which he could easily have done, my march to Bayou Du Lac would have been intercepted and the destruction of my command inevitable.

To have fallen back toward Marksville in order to cover Fort De Russy would equally have insured the disaster. By falling back, however, toward Bayou Du Lac and watching the movements of the enemy I was in hopes of finding an opportunity of attacking him should he march upon Fort De Russy with less than his entire strength. The prairie country through which the enemy would pass would give me an excellent opportunity for observing his movements and estimating his strength. All these considerations induced me to adopt the only course not dictated by folly or madness; and however mortifying it might be to abandon our brave companions in arms at Fort De Russy to their fate, it became my imperative duty to do so rather than attempt assistance, which at best could delay this danger but a few hours, and without a miracle from Heaven would insure the certain destruction of my entire command. I have never had a doubt about the propriety of my course, but do not expect to escape malignant criticisms. If they come from responsible sources I know how to meet them, and only ask that they be made in an open manner.

I commenced my movement to Bayou Du Lac bridge at 10 a.m. on the 14th, and not until the enemy, having repaired the burnt bridge over Bayou De Glaize, had commenced crossing his infantry in force. The road followed by my division diverges from the Marksville and Simsport road at Mansura. We retired leisurely and in perfect order along this road, and except by a body of 60 or 80 of the enemy's cavalry, who drove in on the infantry the few mounted officers who, in default of cavalry, were acting as a cavalry rear guard, our march was uninterrupted.

The enemy, on reaching the intersection of the road on which he was marching and that by which we were retiring, moved straight on to Fort De Russy without halting, his long column well closed up and leaving no stragglers behind. Moving slowly and halting frequently to watch the movements of the enemy, the rear of my column did not reach Bayou Du Lac until 4 p.m.

Confederates at Fort DeRussy:

13th Texas Cavalry

Col. Burnett   W. McClendon   Col. Waller

14th Texas Infantry

Col. Clark   Ellett   Col. Gould

16th Texas Infantry

Cope   Fitzhugh   Col. Flournoy

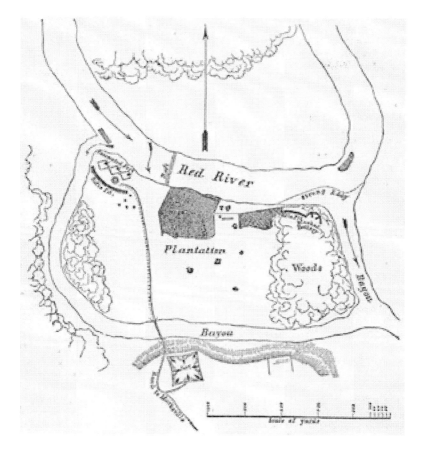

History from National Park Service website:

Early on the morning of the 14th, they continued the march, discovering that a Confederate division threatened their advance. Always mindful of this threat, Smith had to place part of his command in a position to intercept these Rebel forces if they attacked. Upon arriving at the fort, the enemy garrison of 350 men opened fire. Smith decided to use Mower's division, XVI Army Corps, to take the fort and set about positioning it for the attack. Around 6:30 pm, Smith ordered a charge on the fort and about twenty minutes later, Mower's men scaled the parapet, causing the enemy to surrender. Fort DeRussy, which some had said was impregnable, had fallen and the Red River to Alexandria was open.

Confederates at Fort DeRussy:

17th Texas Infantry

Col. R. Allen   *Boydstun*   *Maj. Mabry*   *Mauldin*

Terry   *Thompson*

18th Texas Infantry

Bonner   *Boyce*   *Culbertson*

March 14...Fort DeRussy Falls

In the mean time I had been joined by a company of the Second Louisiana Cavalry and a portion of Faulkner's company, whom I dispatched at once toward Marksville and Mansura to gain information. From the latter direction I learned that the enemy's forces were under the command of Maj. Gen. A. J. Smith, and was a portion of Sherman's late Mississippi expedition, and that their force was about 15,000 infantry, with a large park of artillery. From the direction of Marksville I learned that the enemy's column reached Marksville about 3 o'clock, and that a column of about 4,000 men pushed directly through to Fort De Russy, while the greater portion of the command halted in the immediate vicinity of the village. Later I learned that the fort was invested about 4 p.m., and that a fierce musket and artillery fire was kept up until about sundown, when it ceased, and from the shout of the enemy it was supposed the fort then surrendered.

Up to this time I was in hopes that the holding out of the fort for a day or two would enable me to be re-enforced by Mouton's and Polignac's brigades, when we could have attacked the covering force of the enemy at Marksville, and perhaps raised the siege of Fort De Russy, although even with this re-enforcement the superiority of the enemy would have been too great to give more than the faintest hope of success. Being now satisfied, however, that Fort De Russy had surrendered, it became a matter of the utmost importance for my command to reach the Natchitoches road at this point in advance of the enemy, or otherwise we would necessarily be thrown back into the desert between the Calcasieu and Sabine, when the only escape from starvation would be a hasty retreat into Texas by way of Nib-lett's Bluff. The enemy, having now the control of the river, could re-embark his forces, and removing them rapidly to Alexandria could reach this point by a march of 30 miles, whereas my division, being compelled to make a long detour through the pine woods, could not reach this point in less than four or five days of ordinary marching, it being over 75 miles. Under these circumstances I thought it my duty to take up my line of

Confederates at Fort DeRussy:
19th Texas Infantry

Conner   Hicks   McLean   Peterson   Wallace

22nd Texas Infantry

Richard Hubbard

28th Texas Cavalry

Eli Baxter, Jr.   John Gill   A. B. Irion

march at once without awaiting instructions, which I did about 10 p.m. on the 14th, and on the next morning arrived at Lloyd's Bridge with my whole force, including Mouton's brigade, commanded by Colonel Gray, which I found encamped on the Huffpower, 19 miles south of Fort De Russy, under orders to re-enforce my division.

I was informed by Colonel Gray that he received the order to march to my assistance at 5 p.m. on the 13th, but too late to march that day, having had no previous intimation to be in readiness.

I would respectfully ask the attention of the major-general commanding to these facts and dates, inasmuch as there seems to have been some unaccountable delay, since the information in regard to the landing of the enemy in force reached your headquarters during the night of the 12th, and were acknowledged at 6 o'clock on the next morning, and yet Mouton's brigade received no orders to march until 5 o'clock on the 13th, and did not march until 5 a.m. on the 14th.

Local Militia at Fort DeRussy

Evariste Barre   *Eloi Joffrion*   *Moreau*   *A. Roule*

Louis Roule   D. Siess   S. Siess

March 14, 1864…
Marksville, Mansura & DeRussy

From Diary by Sgt. Charles Ewringmann of the 27th Iowa Infantry

We proceeded into battle and with casualties of about 30 men took into our possession the fort and 11 cannons, 400 prisoners, a quantity of rations and ammunition. We had marched 32 miles that day and by sunset a rather hot days work was done.

There were only French who lived here and many could not speak English. The countryside was outstanding; a great treeless plain 50 miles wide with forest surrounding it; on the edges the people lived in quaint little houses; almost everyone here was a cattlebreeder.

 There they built themselves a little church with a slender steeple sticking out of the treetops of the oaks and on it a golden cupola, glistening white in the sunshine; we passed some convents the same day and the nuns shouted out curiosities from behind iron bars and looked at the passing soldiers with big eyes. The nights were very cold and we froze through completely on the open prairie.

Avoyelles plantation homes target of war

Grimes Bluff antebellum home on Red River across from Dunn's Bayou was damaged during the Civil War. Tillman Grimes, a son of the owner, taught with Union General Sherman at LSU when it began in nearby Pineville just before the war. The home stood until the 1940s.

Another home on Red River which was destroyed during the war was the Ludger Barbin Home, located at Fort DeRussy. It was also two story plantation home. Barbin had allowed the use of his cotton plantation on the bend of the river to be used to build the fort. The house was ransacked and some family heirlooms were scatted along the nearby roads. Barbin rebuilt a smaller home on the same site which stood until the 1960s.

Alexandria, as seen a year earlier during the 1863 Red River campaign.

March 15-16, 1864....Alexandria
Report of U.S. General A. J. Smith

On the evening of the 15th instant I sent Brigadier-General Mower, with the First and Third Divisions, Sixteenth Army Corps, on transports to occupy Alexandria, retaining at Fort De Russy General Thomas Kirby Smith's command, of the Seventeenth Army Corps, for the purpose of dismantling the fort and destroying effectually the magazines and casemates. This was accomplished on the 15th, 16th, and 17th, by tearing down the revetments on the inside of the parapet and digging ditches across the parapet, so that, from the nature of the soil of which it was constructed, the first rain-storm would nearly level it. The magazines, which were bomb-proof and four in number, were totally destroyed by blowing them up with a portion of the powder captured. The casemates were destroyed by piling wood under them and burning them down, the iron bending with the heat. Before they were burned the gun-boat Essex tested their strength with a 100-pounder Parrott at a distance of about 300 yards, firing three shots. The projectile in each case cut through the iron plating, but was stopped by the oak backing. The two 6-

pounder iron guns were also destroyed by bursting. On the morning of the 18th, I left with the remainder of my command for Alexandria, at which place we arrived about 5 p.m. same day.

Report of U.S. General A. J. Smith

General Mower, upon his arrival on the 16th, found the place had been evacuated but a few hours before, the enemy retreating toward Natchitoches. He took possession of three pieces of artillery and some ordnance stores, which the enemy had not time to remove. My instructions being to report to Major-General Banks at this place I disembarked my command and went into camp, he not having arrived.

March 19...Cavalry leads the way

Report of U.S. General A. J. Smith

On the morning of the 19th 100 cavalry, sent forward with dispatches from the advance of the land column of General Banks' command, arrived.

Report of U.S. Major General Nathaniel Banks:

Officers of my staff were at Alexandria on the 19th.

March 20....moving North

Report of U.S. General A. J. Smith

On the 20th, the Cavalry Division of his command, under command of Brig. Gen. A. L. Lee, arrived and went into camp, and the same day Brigadier-General Stone, chief of staff, with a portion of the staff of Major-General Banks, came by river. Learning that a portion of General Dick Taylor's command were in the vicinity of Henderson's Hill, on Bayou Rapides, about 22 miles from Alexandria, on the direct road to Natchitoches,

I directed Brigadier-General Mower to take the First Division, Sixteenth Army Corps, one regiment of infantry and one battery of light artillery from the Third Division, Sixteenth Army Corps, and the First Brigade, Cavalry Division, of General Lee's command, and proceed to

Henderson's Hill, dislodge the enemy from that position, and send forward his cavalry to Red River, clearing all the country between Bayou Rapides and Red River.

March 21, 1864...Alexandria

Report of U.S. Major General Nathaniel Banks:

While at Alexandria Major-General McPherson, commanding at Vicksburg, called for the immediate return of the Marine Brigade--a part of General Smith's command--to protect the Mississippi, for which service it had been specially organized. The transports of this brigade were unable to pass above Alexandria; the hospital-boat Woodford had been wrecked on the rapids in attempting the passage up. The troops were suffering from small-pox, which pervaded all the transports, and they were reported in condition of partial mutiny. It was not supposed at that time that a depot or garrison at Alexandria would be required, and this command, being without available land or water transportation, was permitted to return to the Mississippi, in compliance with the demands of General McPherson. This reduced the strength of the advancing column about 3,000 men.

The condition of the river and the inability of the transports to pass the falls made it necessary to establish a depot of supplies at Alexandria and a line of wagon transportation from the steamers below to those above the falls. This was a departure from the plan of the campaign, which did not contemplate a post or depot at any point on Red River, and involved the necessity of leaving a division at Alexandria for the purpose of protecting the depot, transports, and supplies. Brig. Gen. C. Grover was placed in command of the post, and his division left for its defense. This reduced the force of the advancing column about 3,000 men.

While at Alexandria, on the 21st instant, a movement was organized against the enemy posted at Henderson's Hill, 25 miles in advance. The expedition consisted of three brigades of General A. J. Smith's command and a brigade of cavalry of the Nineteenth Corps, under command of Colonel Lucas, of the Sixteenth Indiana Volunteers, the whole under command of Brigadier-General Mower, of the Sixteenth Corps. The enemy was surprised, losing 250 prisoners, 200 horses, and 4 guns with their caissons. Col. H. B. Sargent, of my staff, was severely wounded in this action, and disabled from service during the campaign. This affair reflected the highest credit upon the officers and men engaged.

Report of U.S. Major General Nathaniel Banks:

Under the general prize law the naval authorities upon their arrival at Alexandria commenced the capture of cotton on both sides of the river, extending their operations from 6 to 10 miles into the interior. Wagon trains were organized, cotton gins put in operation, and the business followed up with great vigor while the fleet lay at Alexandria. Some difficulty occurred with the marines, who insisted upon their right to pass the lines of the army, which was terminated by the advance of the army and navy to Grand Ecore.

I was informed by parties claiming property which had been taken by the naval authorities, to whom I referred them, that, upon application for relief, their property had been released to them by the commander of the fleet. The army did not enter into competition with the navy in the capture of this property.

March 21, 1864...Henderson's Hill
Historical marker at site

Henderson's Hill is located about 3.5 miles southwest of Boyce and 300 feet west of this marker.

At Alexandria, on March 21, 1864, an expedition was organized against the Confederate strong point at Henderson's Hill. This expedition, under the command of Brig. Gen. Mower of the 16th Corps, included three brigades of Gen. A.J. Smith's command and a brigade of cavalry of the 19th Corps under Col. Lucas of the 16th Indiana Volunteers. Confederate forces, which included the 2nd Louisiana Cavalry under the command of Col. William G. Vincent, and William Edgar's battery of light artillery, were surprised by the Federal units. Col. Vincent escaped, but 250 Confederates were captured along with Edgar's four-gun battery. Eight Confederates were killed and one Federal soldier was reported wounded.

Report of U.S. General A. J. Smith

Leaving Alexandria on the morning of the 21st, General Mower reached the vicinity of Henderson's Hill the same night and found it occupied by the enemy with both cavalry and artillery. Leaving three regiments of infantry, one section of the battery, and the cavalry to occupy the attention of the enemy in front, he took two regiments of infantry, one section of the battery, and the Sixteenth Indiana Mounted Infantry and made a detour to the left under cover of the darkness and came in on their rear.

Here, capturing a courier who had been sent from the hill with dispatches for General Dick Taylor, he succeeded in obtaining the countersign, and learning from the dispatches that there was only one regiment of cavalry and one battery of artillery on the hill he moved forward and completely surprised the whole force, capturing them in detail at their camp-fires without a shot being fired. The regiment was the Second Louisiana (rebel) Cavalry, with horses and equipments, and Edgar's battery of light artillery, of four pieces, all complete, the prisoners numbering 262. The detachment making the capture had marched that day over 30 miles through rain and mud.

March 22, 1864...Alexandria
Report of U.S. General A. J. Smith
On the morning of the 22d, General Mower returned with his command to Alexandria.

March 24-26, 1864...Alexandria
Report of U.S. Major General Nathaniel Banks:
... I made my headquarters there (in Alexandria) on the 24th, the forces under General Franklin arriving on the 25th and 26th of March; but as the stage of the water in Red River was too low to admit the passage of the gunboats or transports over the falls, the troops encamped near Alexandria, General Smith and his command moving forward 21 miles to Bayou

Rapides, above Alexandria. There was but 6 feet of water in the channel, while 7 was necessary for the second-class and 10 feet for the first-class gun-boats. The river is narrow, the channel tortuous, changing with every rise, making its navigation more difficult and dangerous probably than any of the Western rivers, while pilots for the transports were reluctant to enter Government service for this campaign.

March 26, 1864...Banks arrives
Report of U.S. General A. J. Smith
On the 26th, General Banks having arrived, I was directed by him to march my command to Cotile Landing and await the arrival of our transports, it being considered dangerous to attempt to take them over the falls with the troops on them.

March 26, 1864...Crossing rapids
Report of U.S. Major General Nathaniel Banks:
The first gun-boat was unable to cross the rapids until the 26th; others crossed on the 28th, with some transports, and others still on the 2d and 3d of April, the passage having been made with difficulty and danger, occupying several days. Several gun-boats and transports, being unable then to ascend the river, remained at Alexandria or returned to the Mississippi.

Grand Ecore during the Civil War, Harper's Weekly

March 28, 1864.... Grand Ecore
Report of U.S. General A. J. Smith

I arrived with the command at Cotile Landing on the 28th; embarked the troops as the transports arrived, and on the 2d of April proceeded up the river, with orders to report to Major-General Banks at Grand Ecore.

General Bank's army, crossing the Cane River, March 31, 1864

April 1, 1864... Alexandria election

Report of U.S. Major General Nathaniel Banks:
On the 1st of April, two or three days before the army moved from Alexandria to Natchitoches, an election of delegates to the constitutional convention was held at Alexandria by request of citizens of the parish of Rapides. No officer or soldier interfered with or had any part whatever in this matter. It was left exclusively to the loyal citizens of the place. Three hundred votes were given in this election, which was a large majority of all the voting population in that parish. Fifteen hundred votes were a full representation of the people before the war. Nearly 500 men from this and neighboring parishes enlisted in the army as mounted scouts, and rendered efficient and valuable services during the campaign.

April 2, 1864...Crump's Corner

April 2nd Brigadier General Albert Lee, commanding the Federal's 5,000-man cavalry division, received a shock from 1,500 Confederates at a crossroads called Crump's Corner near Marthaville.

Although the results were inconclusive Lee was struck by the ferocity of the attack and pronounced that Confederate resistance was stiffening and that could mean only one thing, a major battle was near. William B. Franklin scoffed at that notion, stating the Confederates would continue to fall back until they reached Shreveport.

Crump's Hill was so named because Silas M. Crump of the Marthaville area lived there. He is listed in the 1860 census as S M Crump, 32, native of Alabama.

Grave of the unknown soldier near Crump's Hill

Unknown Red River Rebel

Perhaps the most celebrated soldier of the Red River Campaign today is the unknown soldier who's remembered at the Rebel State Park near Marthaville, Natchitoches Parish. According to a local legend, this young Confederate soldier became separated from his unit and shortly after he stopped at a spring for a drink of water the lad was spotted by three Union cavalrymen and killed.

The Barnhill family, local residents who had spoken with the soldier shortly before he was shot, discovered his body and buried him beside the road where he had died.

In 1962, area residents placed a marker on the spot and began to hold annual memorial services in honor of the Unknown Confederate Soldier. From that the Rebel State Historic Site has been established at this soldier's final resting place. An annual concert pays tribute not only to the soldier but to the kindness of the people of Natchitoches Parish.

19th Union Army crossing Cane River in Natchitoches Parish

April 2, 1864...Natchitoches

Report of U.S. Major General Nathaniel Banks:
    Anticipating by a few days the passage of the gunboats, the army marched from Alexandria for Natchitoches, 80 miles distant by land, reaching that point on the 2d and 3d of April. The enemy continued his retreat, skirmishing sharply with the advanced guard, but offering no serious resistance to our advance. The shortest and only practicable road from Natchitoches to Shreveport was the stage road through Pleasant Hill and Mansfield (distance 100 miles), through a barren, sandy country, with little water and less forage, the greater portion an unbroken pine forest.
    A reconnaissance from Natchitoches on the 2d of April, under command of General Lee, discovered the enemy in force at Pleasant Hill, 36 miles distant, and established the fact that a portion of Green's command had arrived from Texas, and were then confronting us. Prisoners captured from Price's command indicated (what had been feared from the loss of time at Alexandria) a concentration of the entire available force of the enemy, numbering, according to the statements of prisoners and intercepted letters, about 25,000 men, with seventy-six guns.
    The river was perceptibly falling, and the larger gun-

boats were unable to pass Grand Ecore. The troops, under command of General A. J. Smith, had hitherto moved in transports by the river, now marched by land from Natchitoches, with the exception of one division of the Seventeenth Corps, 2,500 men, under Brig. Gen. T. Kirby Smith, which, by order of General A. J. Smith, continued its movements by the river, in company with the fleet, for the protection of the transports. The arrangement of land transportation for this portion of the column, the replenishing of supply trains from the transports, and the distribution of rations to the troops were made at this point, but the fleet was unable to ascend the river until the 7th of April. The condition of the river would have justified the suspension of the movement altogether at either point, except for the anticipation of such a change as to render it navigable. Upon this subject the counsel of the naval officers was implicitly followed.

Union Admiral Porter

April 2, 1864...Natchitoches

Peter Tubbs. He was a private in Company I, 29th Regiment, Wisconsin Infantry, writing letters home to his sister Sarah Jane Merrell of Neosho,

He wrote:
On April 2, 1864, from Natchitoches, La., he wrote: "We are getting into the country where there are more negroes than there has been and they think they are surely delivered from bondage. They are our only friends. ... They seem to be willing to divide the last mouthful with the soldiers. ... They are perfectly delighted with the musik (and) some of them will dance as long as they can hear it."

1864, April   Porter Flotilla on Red River at Alexandria preparing to go upriver.

April 3, 1864...Grand Ecore

Report of U.S. General A. J. Smith

    Arrived at Grand Ecore on the 3d, and was ordered by Major-General Banks to be in readiness to leave for Shreveport by land on the 7th instant, and to send the transports with all surplus subsistence stores, baggage, etc., with sufficient guard, by water to the mouth of Loggy Bayou; at that point to await further orders. I accordingly detached Brig. Gen. Thomas Kirby Smith with his Seventeenth Corps for duty with the boats, and directed him to consult with Admiral Porter as to the time and manner of starting. I left with the two divisions of the Sixteenth Corps on the 7th instant, bringing up the rear of the land column. General T. Kirby Smith also left on the same day with the transports, and his report of this part of the expedition is herewith submitted. Moving toward Pleasant Hill in the rear of the land column, the trains of the cavalry, Thirteenth, and Sixteenth Corps, all being in front of me, and the roads very bad, my progress was consequently slow. We kept well closed up, however, on the train, and encamped on the night of the 7th about 8 miles from Grand Ecore.

April 4, 1864...Keachie-Mansfield
Report of General Kirby Smith, C.S.A.
On April 4, Churchill's and Parsons' divisions were ordered to Keachie, within supporting distance of General Taylor, at Mansfield.

April 4, 1864...Cavalry attack
Report of U.S. Major General Nathaniel Banks:
On the 4th of April, Col. O. P. Gooding, commanding a brigade of cavalry engaged upon a reconnaissance north of Red River, encountered Harrison's command, 1,500 strong, in which the enemy was defeated with considerable loss. Our loss was about 40 in killed, wounded, and missing. The enemy's repulse was decisive.

April 5, 1864...Mansfield
Report of General Kirby Smith, C.S.A.
On the morning of April 5, I repaired to General Taylor's headquarters at Mansfield, and on the afternoon of same day returned to Shreveport, from which point the operations of Generals Price and Taylor's commands could best be directed.

In my interview with General Taylor at Mansfield on April 5, my plan of operations was distinctly explained. He agreed with me and expressed his belief that General Steele, being the bolder and more active, would advance sooner and more rapidly than Banks, and was the column first to be attacked.

April 6, 1864...Head for Shreveport
Report of U.S. Major General Nathaniel Banks:
The army was put in motion for Shreveport, via Pleasant Hill and Mansfield, April 6. General Lee, with the cavalry division, led the advance, followed by a detachment of two divisions of the Thirteenth Corps, under General Ransom; First Division, Nineteenth Corps, under General Emory, and a brigade of colored troops under command of Colonel Dickey, the whole under the immediate command of Major-General Franklin.

Wilson's Plantation near Pleasant Hill, April 7th. 1864.

April 7, 1864...Leggy Bayou

Report of U.S. Major General Nathaniel Banks:
The detachments of the Sixteenth Army Corps, under command of Brig. Gen. A.J. Smith, followed on the 7th, and a division of the Seventeenth Army Corps, under Brig. Gen. T. Kirby Smith, accompanying Admiral Porter on the river as a guard for the transports. The fleet was directed to Leggy Bayou, opposite Springfield, where it was expected communications would be established with the land forces at Sabine Cross-Roads, a distance of 54 miles by land from Grand Ecore, and 100 miles by water.

    I remained with a portion of my staff to superintend the departure of the river and land forces from Grand Ecore until the morning of the 7th and then rode rapidly forward, reaching the head of the column at Pleasant Hill the same evening, where the main body encamped. General Smith s command was at the rear of the column on the march, but passed the negro brigade on the route to Pleasant Hill. A very heavy rain fell all day on the 7th, which greatly impeded the movement of the rear of the column, making the road almost impassable for troops, trains, or artillery. The storm did not reach the head of the column. In passing the troops from Natchitoches to Pleasant Hill I endeavored as much as possible to accelerate their movements. The enemy offered no opposition to their march on the 6th. On the 7th, the advance drove a small force to Pleasant Hill, and from there to Wilson's farm, 3 miles beyond, where a sharp fight occurred with the enemy posted in a very strong position, from which they were driven with serious loss and pursued to Saint Patrick s Bayou, near Carroll's Mill, about 9 miles from Pleasant Hill, where our forces bivouacked for the night. We sustained in this action a loss of 14 men killed, 39 wounded, and 9 missing. We captured many prisoners and the enemy sustained severe losses in killed and wounded. During the action General Lee sent to General Franklin for re-enforcements, and a brigade of infantry was sent forward, but the firing having ceased it was withdrawn. The officers and men fought with great spirit in this affair.

April 8, 1864...Battle of Mansfield

Report of General Kirby Smith, C.S.A.

General Taylor having reported the advance of the enemy's cavalry to Pleasant Hill, on the morning of April 8, I wrote him the inclosed letter (numbered 2595). His headquarters was between four and five hours by courier from Shreveport. The action was unexpectedly brought on by Mouton engaging the enemy at 5 o'clock in the evening of April 8.

Report of U.S. General A. J. Smith

Moving forward at daylight on the morning of the 8th, we encamped at night about 2 miles from Pleasant Hill, having marched about 21 miles. Heard heavy cannonading in front during the afternoon, and sent forward word to General Banks my exact position, and also stated that if he desired I could pass the train with a portion or all of my command. Soon after I learned that the cause of the cannonading was an attack by the enemy upon the cavalry and the Thirteenth Army Corps, which were in the advance about 8 miles beyond Pleasant Hill, and whom the enemy had repulsed and totally routed, capturing their artillery and wagons, and with a loss of nearly one-half the Thirteenth Corps, and that the enemy were only checked by night and the Nineteenth Corps. Ordering my men to bivouac upon their arms, and throwing out pickets to their flanks and rear, we rested until morning, when, by permission of General Banks, I moved forward to, Pleasant Hill and formed line of battle across the Mansfield road. During the night and morning the remaining and disorganized parties of the cavalry and Thirteenth Army Corps arriving, passed through the lines and halted.

...April 8, 1864...Battle of Mansfield

Report of U.S. Major General Nathaniel Banks:
At daybreak on the 8th, General Lee, to whose support a brigade of the Thirteenth Corps, under Colonel Landram, had been sent by my order, advanced upon the enemy, drove him from his position on the opposite side of Saint Patrick's Bayou, and pursued him to Sabine Cross-Roads, about 3 miles from Mansfield. The advance was steady but slow, and the resistance of the enemy stubborn. He was only driven from his defensive positions on the road by artillery. At noon on the 8th, another brigade of the Thirteenth Corps arrived at the crossroads under Brigadier-General Ransom to relieve the First Brigade.

    The infantry moved from Pleasant Hill at daybreak on the 8th, the head of the column halting at Saint Patrick's Bayou in order that the rear might come up. I passed General Franklin's headquarters at 10 a.m., giving directions to close up the column as speedily as possible, and rode forward to ascertain the condition of affairs at the front, where I arrived between I and 2 o'clock. General Ransom arrived nearly at the same time, with the Second Brigade, Thirteenth Corps, which was under his command in the action at the cross-roads. I found the troops in line of battle, the skirmishers sharply engaged, the main body of the enemy posted on the crest of a hill in thick woods on both sides of a road leading over the hill to Mansfield on our line of march. It was apparent that the enemy was in much stronger force than at any previous point on the march, and being confirmed in this opinion by General Lee, I sent to General Franklin, immediately upon my arrival, a statement of the facts and orders to hurry forward the infantry with all possible dispatch, directing General Lee at the same time to hold his ground steadily, but not advance until re-enforcements should arrive. Our forces were for a long time stationary, with some skirmishing on the flanks. It soon became apparent that the entire force of the enemy was in our front. Several officers were sent to General Franklin to hurry forward the column. Skirmishing was incessant during the afternoon. At 4.30 p.m. the enemy made a general attack all along the lines, but with great vigor upon our right flank. It was resisted with resolute determination by our troops, but overpowering numbers compelled them, after resisting the successive charges of the enemy in front and on the flank, to fall back from their position to the woods in rear of the open field, which they occupied, retreating in good order. The enemy pressed with great vigor upon the flanks, as well as in front, for the purpose of getting to the rear, but were repulsed in this attempt by our cavalry.

At the line of woods a new position was assumed, supported by the Third Division of the Thirteenth Army Corps, under General Cameron, which reached this point about 5 p.m., and formed in line of battle under the direction of Major-General Franklin, who accompanied its advance. The enemy attacked this second line with great impetuosity and overpowering numbers, turning both flanks and advancing heavily upon the center. The assault was resisted with gallantry, but the troops, finding the enemy in the rear, were compelled to yield the ground and fall steadily back. The road was badly obstructed by the supply train of the cavalry division, which prevented the retreat of both men and artillery. We lost ten of the guns of Ransom's division in consequence of the position of the train, which prevented their withdrawal. Repeated efforts were made to reform the troops and resist the advance of the enemy, but though their progress was checked, it was without permanent success.

1864 Battle of Mansfield

...April 8, 1864...Battle of Mansfield

Brig. Gen. W. H. Emory, commanding First Division, Nineteenth Corps, had been early notified of the condition of affairs, and directed to advance as rapidly as possible and form a line of battle in the strongest position he could select, to support the troops in retreat and check the advance of the enemy. The order to advance found him 7 miles to the rear of the first battle-ground. He assumed a position at Pleasant Grove, about 3 miles from the cross-roads, on the edge of the woods commanding an open field, sloping to the front. The One hundred and sixty-first New York Volunteers, Lieutenant-Colonel Kinsey commanding, were deployed as skirmishers and ordered to the foot of the hill, upon the crest of which the line was formed to cover the rear of the retreating forces, to check the pursuit of the enemy, and give time for the formation of the troops.

General Dwight, commanding First Brigade, formed his troops across the road upon which the enemy was moving, commanding the open field in front. The Third Brigade, Colonel Benedict commanding, formed to the left, and the Second Brigade, General McMillan, in reserve. The line was scarcely formed when the One hundred and sixty-first New York Volunteers were attacked and driven in. The right being threatened, a portion of McMillan's brigade formed on the right of General Dwight. The fire of our troops was reserved until the enemy was at close quarters, when the whole line opened upon them with most destructive volleys of musketry. The action lasted an hour and a half. The enemy was repulsed with very great slaughter. During the fight a determined effort was made to turn our left flank, which was defeated. Prisoners reported the loss of the enemy in officers and men to be very great.

General Mouton was killed in the first onset. Their attack was made with great desperation, apparently with the idea that the dispersion of our forces at this point would end the campaign, and with the aid of the steadily falling river leave the fleet of transports and gun-boats in their hands or compel their destruction. Nothing could surpass in impetuosity the assault of the enemy but the inflexible steadiness and valor of our troops. The First Division of the Nineteenth Corps, by its great bravery in this action, saved the army and navy. But for this successful resistance to the attack of the enemy at Pleasant Grove, the renewed attack of the enemy with increased force could not have been successfully resisted at Pleasant Hill on the 9th of April. We occupied both battlegrounds at night.

From Pleasant Grove, where this action occurred, to Pleasant Hill was 15 miles. It was certain that the enemy, who was within the reach of re-enforcements, would renew the attack in the morning, and it was wholly uncertain whether the command of General Smith could reach the position we held in season for a second engagement. For this reason the army toward morning fell back to Pleasant Hill, General Emory covering the rear, burying the dead, bringing off the wounded, and all the material of the army. It arrived there at 8.30 on the morning of the 9th, effecting a junction with the forces of General Smith and the colored brigade under Colonel Dickey, which had reached that point the evening previous.

Early on the 9th, the troops were prepared for action, the movements of the enemy indicating that he was on our rear. A line of battle was formed in the following order: First Brigade, Nineteenth Corps, on the right, resting on a ravine; Second Brigade in the center, and Third Brigade on the left. The center was strengthened by a brigade of General Smith's forces, whose main force was held in reserve. The enemy moved toward our right flank. The Second Brigade withdrew from the center to the support of the First Brigade. The brigade in support of the center moved up into position, and another of General Smith's brigades was posted to the extreme left position on the hill, in echelon to the rear of the left main line.

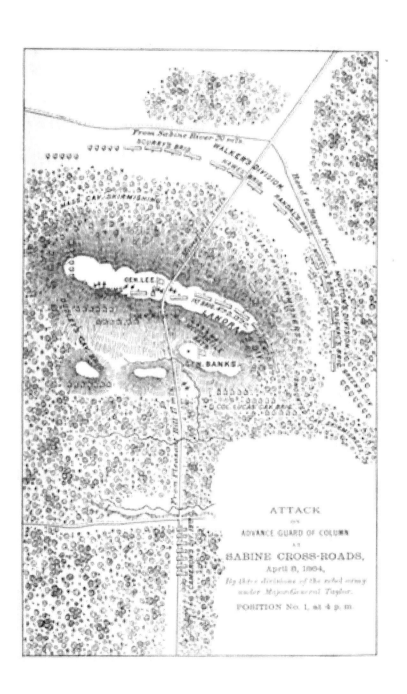

Light skirmishing occurred during the afternoon. Between 4 and 5 o'clock it increased in vigor, and about 5 p.m., when it appeared to have nearly ceased, the enemy drove in our skirmishers and attacked in force, his first onset being against the left. He advanced in two oblique lines, extending well over toward the right of the Third Brigade, Nineteenth Corps. After a determined resistance this part of the line gave way and went slowly back to the reserves. The First and Second Brigades were soon enveloped in front, right, and rear. By skillful movements of General Emory the flanks of the two brigades, now bearing the brunt of the battle, were covered. The enemy pursued the brigades, passing the left and center, until he approached the reserves under General Smith, when he was met by a charge led by General Mower and checked. The whole of the reserves were now ordered up, and in turn we drove the enemy, continuing the pursuit until night compelled us to halt.

Rebels attack Gen, Albert Lee's Wagon Train near Mansfield.

Some of the men lost at Mansfield

Gen. Mouton, Capt. de la garza, Maj. Gen. Polignac

James Beard,   Sgt., Leopold Armant   Capt. Elijah Parsons

Capt. W. Fuller   Oneal Manuel, April 8   Lt. John Francis

April 9, 1864...Pleasant Hill
Report of General Kirby Smith, C.S.A.

I received General Taylor's dispatch announcing the engagement at 4 o'clock on the morning of April 9, and rode 65 miles that day to Pleasant Hill, but did not reach there in time for the battle, which opened at 4 o'clock in the afternoon.

Early in the morning they, with the trains, were ordered to proceed immediately to Grand Ecore, leaving on the field part of the Nineteenth and two divisions of the Sixteenth Army Corps.

Line of battle was formed as follows: First Brigade of General Emory's command of the Nineteenth Corps on the extreme right and right flank, the Third and First Divisions, Sixteenth Army Corps, on the right and left center, and the remaining troops of the Thirteenth Corps on the extreme left and left flank, my right lapping a brigade on Emory's left and about 400 yards in its rear. The Second Brigade, Third Division, Col. William T. Shaw commanding, was ordered early in the morning to report to Brigadier-General Emory, and was stationed in front of the center of his command.

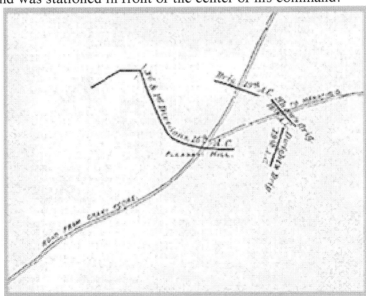

The enemy's skirmishers appeared on Colonel Shaw's front about noon, and there was desultory skirmishing at different parts of the line until about 4.30 p.m., when the enemy made his attack on the right center, driving in the outposts and the brigade of the Nineteenth Corps in my front through my line, they reforming in my rear. Advancing my line slightly to be able to close with and support Shaw's brigade, the battle immediately became general. The enemy had been re-enforced during the afternoon with two divisions of infantry from Price's command, and their troops, flushed with their success of the previous day, seemed determined to break through our line, charging it with desperate energy. Fearing that Shaw's brigade might be totally enveloped, I directed him to fall back and connect with my right. In the mean time the enemy's right had advanced beyond my extreme left and were taken in flank and rolled up by the First Brigade, Third Division, Col. William F. Lynch commanding. Seizing the opportunity I ordered a charge by the whole line, and we drove them back, desperately fighting, step by step across the field, through the wood, and into the open field beyond, fully a mile from the battle-field, when they took advantage of the darkness and fell back toward Mansfield thoroughly whipped and demoralized. In the charge we captured nearly 1,000 prisoners, five pieces of artillery, and six caissons. The artillery was brought off, but the caissons were left until morning. The casualties in my command were as follows: Killed, 98; wounded, 529; missing, 124; total, 751. A large proportion of the missing were of the Thirty-second Iowa, which was on the left of Shaw's brigade, and were nearly surrounded in the early part of the battle during the enemy's first charge. The loss of the enemy in killed was unusually severe.

A brigade of cavalry which charged Shaw's brigade in the early part of the action were almost annihilated, he allowing them to approach within 50 yards before opening fire. The prisoners captured were many of them from Missouri regiments, belonging to the divisions that had re-enforced the enemy during the engagement. The darkness compelled us to cease pursuit.

Anticipating the order to follow up our success by a vigorous pursuit, the next morning I sent the Third Brigade,

...April 9, 1864...Pleasant Hill

Third Division, Col. R. M. Moore commanding, about 2 miles out on the road taken by the retreating enemy, with orders to watch their movements and gain all the information possible, and fell back with the remainder of my command and bivouacked in line on the field of battle. The opinion of Major-General Banks as to the action of the command and its results may be gathered from his own words to me on the field just after the final charge, when, riding up to me, he remarked, shaking me by the hand, "God bless you, general; you have saved the army."

About 12 o'clock on the night of the 9th, I received orders from General Banks to have my command in readiness to move at 2 o'clock in the morning, and at that hour to withdraw them silently from the field and follow the Nineteenth Army Corps back to Grand Ecore, making such disposition of my troops and trains as would enable me to repel an attack on the rear of the column. I represented to him that the dead of my command were not buried, and that I had not the means of transporting my wounded; that many of the wounded had not yet been gathered in from the field, and asked of him permission to remain until noon the next day to give me an opportunity to bury my dead and leave the wounded as well provided for as the circumstances would permit. I also urged the fact that General Thomas Kirby Smith's command, then 30 miles above us on transports in the river, would undoubtedly be captured and the transports lost if left to themselves. The permission to remain was, however, refused and the order to move made peremptory. I therefore provided as well as possible for the wounded, left medical officers to attend to them, and moved at the designated hour, following the Nineteenth Corps. We reached Grand Ecore on the evening of the 11th, no attack on the rear having been made by the enemy, and went into camp. On the evening of the 13th, nothing having been heard from a portion of our transports save that they had been attacked with infantry and artillery upon both sides of the river, I marched up with two brigades of my command on the north bank of the river to help them through, if possible, crossing the river at Grand Ecore at about 4 p.m. We reached Campti, 12 miles above, the same night and met a portion of the fleet there, they having by energy, good judgment, and rare good fortune succeeded in running the batteries and land forces of the enemy without the loss of a boat, though some were completely riddled with shot. The report of Brig. Gen. T.

Some of men lost in Desoto Parish

Sgt. *Byrne,*   *Brig Gen Green*   *Lt. Col. W. Scurry*   *Col. Buchel*
Killed April 9   *Killed April 12*   *Killed April 30*   *Killed April 9*

Battle of Pleasant Hill as seen in Frank Leslie's Illustrated, 1864

Kirby Smith accompanies this, and you are also respectfully referred to the report of Rear-Admiral D.D. Porter, already on file.

Report of U.S. Major General Nathaniel Banks:

The battle of the 9th was desperate and sanguinary. The defeat of the enemy was complete, and his loss in officers and men more than double that sustained by our forces. There was nothing in the immediate position or condition of the two armies to prevent a forward movement the next morning, and orders were given to prepare for an advance. The train, which had been turned to the rear on the day of the battle, was ordered to reform and advance at daybreak. I communicated this purpose at the close of the day to General A. J. Smith, who expressed his concurrence therein. But representations subsequently received from General Franklin and all the general officers of the Nineteenth Corps, as to the condition of their respective commands for immediate active operations against the enemy, caused a suspension of this order, and a conference of the general officers was held in the evening, in which it was determined, upon the urgent recommendation of all the general officers above named, and with the acquiescence of General Smith, to retire upon Grand Ecore the following day. The reasons urged for this course by the officers commanding the Nineteenth and Thirteenth Corps were, first, that the absence of water made it absolutely necessary to advance or retire without delay. General Emory's command had been without rations for two days, and the train, which had been turned to the rear during the battle, could not be put in condition to move forward upon the single road through dense woods, in which it stood, without difficulty and loss of time. It was for the purpose of communicating with the fleet at Springfield Landing from the Sabine Cross-Roads to the river, as well as to prevent the concentration of the Texan troops with the enemy at Mansfield, that we had pushed for the early occupation of that point. Considering the difficulty with which the gun-boats passed Alexandria and Grand Ecore, there was every reason to believe that the navigation of the river would be found impracticable. A squadron of cavalry, under direction of Mr. Young, who had formerly been employed in the surveys of this country and was now connected with the engineer

...April 9, 1864...Pleasant Hill

department, which had been sent upon a reconnaissance to the river, returned to Pleasant Hill on the day of the battle with the report that they had not been able to discover the fleet nor learn from the people its passage up the river. (The report of General T. Kirby Smith, commanding the river forces, states that the fleet did not arrive at Loggy Bayou until 2 p.m. on the 10th of April, two days after the battle at Sabine Cross-Roads.) This led to the belief that the low water had prevented the advance of the fleet. The condition of the river, which had been steadily falling since our march from Alexandria, rendered it very doubtful, if the fleet ascended the river, whether it could return from any intermediate point, and probable, if not certain, that if it reached Shreveport it would never escape without a rise of the river, of which all hopes began to fail. The forces designated for this campaign numbered 42,000 men. Less than half that number was actually available for service against the enemy during its progress.

The distance which separated General Steele's command from the line of our operations (nearly 200 miles) rendered his movements of little moment to us or to the enemy, and reduced the strength of the fighting column to the extent of his force, which was expected to be from 10,000 to 15,000 men. The depot at Alexandria, made necessary by the impracticable navigation, withdrew from our forces 3,000 men under General Grover. The return of the Marine Brigade to the defense of the Mississippi, upon the demand of Major-General McPherson, and which could not pass Alexandria without its steamers nor move by land for want of land transportation, made a further reduction of 3,000 men. The protection of the fleet of transports against the enemy on both sides of the river made it necessary for General A. J. Smith to detach General T. Kirby Smith's division of 2,500 men from the main body for that duty. The army train required a guard of 500 men. These several detachments, which it was impossible to avoid, and the distance of General Steele's command, which it was not in my power to correct, reduced the number of troops that we were able at any point to bring into action from 42,000 men to about 20,000. The losses sustained in the very severe battles of the 7th, 8th, and 9th of

Some soldiers of the 18th Louisiana

Hyp. Arceneaux   Gervais Bordelon   Gus. Bourgeois   Sost. Broussard
Lafayette Parish   Avoyelles Parish   St. James Parish   St Landry Par.

Vict. Brouillette   S. Callegari   M. Chenevert   Anatole Coco
Avoyelles   Avoyelles   Avoyelles   Avoyelles

Leo Champagne   Tom Chase   Joseph Collins   John M. Dick
St. Martin Par.   Caddo Parish   Lt. Colonel   Co. B

Sgt. Grisamore   Steven Fuqua   Capt. Garland   J. V. Guidry
Lacourche   Avoyelles   Co. B   Iberville Parish

Infantry who may have served at Mansfield

Judge W. Hall   Sheriff J. Hayes   F. Hymel   August Hodges
Avoyelles   *St. Landry*   *St. James Parish*   *Calcasieu Parish*

R. C. Landry   Theo. Lemoine   Sgt. A. Moss   Luc Normand
Lafayettte Par   *Avoyelles*   *Lafayette*   Avoyelles

Judge Felix Poche   J. L. Prejean   J. Prudhomme   Aug. Roger
LA Supreme Court   *Lafayette Parish*   *Natchitoches*   *Lafourche Par*

Col. A. Roman   W. M. Rothery   T. Thibodeaux   Jeff Young
St. James Par. Co. B   *St. Martin Par.*   *Beauregard Parish*

April amounted to about 3,969 men, and necessarily reduced our active forces to that extent.

The enemy, superior to us in numbers in the outset, by falling back was able to recover from his great losses by means of re-enforcements, which were within his reach as he approached his base of operations, while we were growing weaker as we departed from ours. We had fought the battle at Pleasant Hill with about 15,000 against 22,000 men and won a victory, which for these reasons we were unable to follow up. Other considerations connected with the actual military condition of affairs afforded additional reasons for the course recommended. Between the commencement of the expedition and the battle of Pleasant Hill a change had occurred in the general command of the army, which caused a modification of my instructions in regard to this expedition.

Lieutenant-General Grant, in a dispatch dated the 15th March, which I received on the 27th March, at Alexandria, eight days before we reached Grand Ecore, by special messenger, gave me the following instructions:

Should you find that the taking of Shreveport will occupy ten or fifteen days more time than General Sherman gave his troops to be absent from their command you will send them back at the time specified in his note of (blank date) March, even if it should lead to the abandonment of the main object of the expedition. Should it prove successful, hold Shreveport and Red River with such force as you deem necessary and return the balance of your troops to the neighborhood of New Orleans.

These instructions, I was informed, were given for the purpose of having "all parts of the army, or rather all armies, act as much in concert as possible," and with a view to a movement in the spring campaign against Mobile, which was certainly to be made "if troops enough could be obtained without embarrassing other movements; in which event New Orleans would be the point of departure for such an expedition." A subsequent dispatch, though it did not control, fully justified my action, repeated these general views and stated that the commanding general "would much rather the Red River expedition had never been begun that that you should be detained one day beyond the 1st of May in commencing the movement east of the Mississippi."

Some of the Consolidated Crescent Regiment who served at Pleasant Hill

Sosth. Baillio W. Brasher Corp. Carroll Corp. J Dabbs
Rapides *Rapides* *Desoto Parish* Ouachita Parish

Pvt J.R. Parrott Matt Edwards Pvt. Matlock Harrison Nash
Sabine Parish *Avoyelles* *Bossier Parish* *Rapides Parish*

Pvt. C.Rowell Capt.W.Spencer Pvt. J Thomas Dr. G. Wise
Bienville Par. *Catahoula Par.* *Natchitoches Pr.* *Claiborne Par.*

...April 9, 1864...Pleasant Hill

  The limitation of time referred to in these dispatches was based upon an opinion which I had verbally expressed to General Sherman at New Orleans, that General Smith could be spared in thirty days after we reached Alexandria, but it was predicted upon the expectation that the navigation of the river would be unobstructed; that we should advance without delay at Alexandria, Grand Ecore, or elsewhere on account of low water, and that the forces of General Steele were to co-operate with us effectively at some point on Red River, near Natchitoches or Monroe. It was never understood that an expedition that involved on the part of my command a land march of nearly 400 miles into the enemy's country, and which terminated at a point which we might not be able to hold, either on account of the strength of the enemy or the difficulties of obtaining supplies, was to be limited to thirty days. The condition of our forces, and the distance and difficulties attending the further advance into the enemy's country after the battles of the 8th and 9th against an enemy superior in numbers to our own, rendered it probable that we could not occupy Shreveport within the time specified, and certain that without a rise in the river the troops necessary to hold it against the enemy would be compelled to evacuate it for want of supplies, and impossible that the expedition should return in any event to New Orleans in time to co-operate in the general movements of the army contemplated for the spring campaign. It was known at this time that the fleet could not repass the rapids at Alexandria, and it was doubtful, if the fleet reached any point above Grand Ecore, whether it would be able to return. By falling back to Grand Ecore we should be able to ascertain the condition of the fleet, the practicability of continuing the movement by the river, reorganize a part of the forces that had been shattered in the battles of the 7th, 8th, and 9th, possibly ascertain the position of General Steele and obtain from him the assistance expected for a new advance north of the river or upon its southern bank, and perhaps obtain definite instructions from the Government as to the course to be pursued.
  Upon these general considerations, and without reference to the actual condition of the respective armies, at

12 o'clock midnight on the 9th I countermanded the order for the return of the train, and directed preparations to be made for the return of the army to Grand Ecore. The dead were buried and the wounded brought in from the field of battle and placed in the most comfortable hospitals that could be provided, and surgeons and supplies furnished for them. A second squadron of cavalry was sent, under direction of Mr. Young, of the engineer department, to inform the fleet of our retrograde movement and to direct its return, if it had ascended the river, and on the morning of the 10th the army leisurely returned to Grand Ecore. The wounded were immediately visited by Dr. Sanger, who took with him clothing, rations, medicines, and other supplies, and reported them in comfortable condition.

A Confederate charge at the Battle of Pleasant Hill. From Harper's Weekly, May 7, 1864.

April 10, 1864...Banks in retreat

Report of General Kirby Smith, C.S.A.

On April 10, General Taylor returned with me to Mansfield, where the further operations of the campaign were discussed and determined upon by us. Banks was in full retreat, with the cavalry in pursuit. Our infantry was withdrawn by General Taylor to Mansfield for supplies. The country below Natchitoches had been completely desolated and stripped of supplies. The navigation of the river was obstructed, and even had our whole force been available for pursuit it could not have been subsisted below Natchitoches. General Steele was advancing, and to have pushed our whole force in pursuit of a fleeing enemy, while Steele's column was in position to march upon our base and destroy our depots and shops, would have been sacrificing the advantages of our central position and abandoning the plan of campaign at the very time we were in position to have insured its success.

General Taylor agreed with me that the main body of our infantry should be pushed against Steele, and requested that he might accompany the column moving to Arkansas. He selected the troops that were to remain, placed General Polignac in command, and gave him his instructions for pushing the retreating army of General Banks.

April 10-12, 1864...
Report of U.S. Major General Nathaniel Banks:

The fleet sailed from Grand Ecore on the 7th and reached its destination at Loggy Bayou on the evening of the 10th, one day after the battle at Pleasant Hill and two days after the engagement at Sabine Cross-Roads. General T. Kirby Smith received a verbal message the evening of the 10th, and on the morning of the 11th written orders to return. The transports were in a crippled condition, rudders unshipped and wheels broken. The enemy attacked the fleet on its return near Pleasant Hill Landing on the 12th, with a force of 2,500 cavalry, a strong reserve infantry, and a battery of six guns, under General Green, but the troops, protected by cotton bales and bales of hay, with the gun-boats, kept up a deadly fire, and drove the enemy from the river. For two miles the bank was strewn with the wounded and dead. Among other rebels officers killed was General Green, who was left dead upon the field. The troops of the transports saw him fall, and claim that his death was the work of their artillery, the gun-boats and transports all firing at the same time. The enemy, under Lid-dell, who had occupied the north bank of the river with 2,500 men, attacked the fleet on the 13th, but was driven back with loss.

The navigation up and down the river was intricate and difficult, and the steamers were frequently aground. Several of the boats were laden with ammunition and ordnance stores, but the energy of the officers and men brought off every boat. The only loss in stores was a hundred sacks of oats, thrown overboard for the relief of a steamer aground. They reached Campti on the 14th, with a loss of 1 man killed and 18 wounded, where they met a force from the army sent to their assistance, and reached Grand Ecore on the 15th without further obstruction.

General T. Kirby Smith, to whose courtesy I am indebted for all the official information I have received of this part of the expedition, mentions with commendation Maj. D.C. Houston, of the engineers, who had in charge the ordnance stores, and Lieut. Col. W. S. Abert, officers of my staff, who accompanied him, and also officers and men of his own command and masters of transport steamers. General Smith, who commanded the land forces and transports, is entitled to the highest commendation for the energy, skill, and success with which he managed this most difficult affair. Lines of defense were established at Grand Ecore the 12th of April, and orders given to attack the enemy if he approached. A pontoon bridge was thrown across the river during the night. Our pickets were driven in on the 13th, but the enemy appeared, upon a reconnaissance made in force, to have gone below for the purpose either of attacking our troops at Alexandria or occupying Monett's Bluff, on Cane River. On the same day General Smith crossed the river with two brigades, two batteries, and a strong cavalry force, to aid the fleet still above Grand Ecore. Dispatches were sent to General Steele informing him of the condition of affairs, and requesting him to join us at some point on the river. Orders were sent to New Orleans for re-enforcements, and the lieutenant-general commanding the Army was informed of the condition of affairs by telegraph and of my intention to advance upon Shreveport, if General Steele could come to our assistance, and my determination not to withdraw without orders.

April 12, 1864: *newspaper report*

GALVESTON WEEKLY NEWS, May 4, 1864, p. 1, c. 5-6
Under date of April 12th, Capt. Boren*, of this place, writes to his sister (says the Tyler Reporter) as follows: . . .
"Prisoners are being brought in every day.—Before Banks gets his army safe under the shot and shell of his gunboats, we will capture not less than five thousand.
"They will all be sent to Texas, and in all probability to Tyler. If they are sent to Tyler, I wish they may receive just such treatment as Confederate States soldiers have at their hands. I could not regret their death by starvation, for as they came up from Alexandria they devastated the whole country.

All live stock, and all provision of every description, were taken from helpless women and children. Their furniture was burnt and broken up. Beds and every article of clothing was taken or destroyed. Ladies told me that the Yankees acted so much like fiends, that they were compelled to seek refuge in the woods, where they remained two days and nights."
*Captain A. B. Boren, Co. "K" 35th (Likens) Texas Cavalry Regt, CSA

Transcribed by William J. Bozic, Jr., Houston, TX

April 14, 1864
Report of U.S. General A. J. Smith
On the 14th, I returned to Grand Ecore with the rear of the fleet.

Pursuant to orders from Major-General Banks, after placing a proper guard on each of my transports, with directions for them to proceed down the river to Alexandria, I moved with the remainder of my command on the 20th to Natchitoches. Occupying this place as *a point de resistance* with my troops, the remainder of General Banks' forces passed between us and the river, continuing the retreat to Alexandria.

April 15, 1864...
Report of U.S. Major General Nathaniel Banks:

The fleet returned on the 15th in safety, without loss of vessels or material of war. Admiral Porter, with whom I had a conference on his arrival at Grand Ecore, advised against any further attempt to advance without a rise of the river, and his counsel was followed. The river had been steadily falling. Supplies were brought up to Grand Ecore with very great difficulty. It was found that two of the gun-boats could not go below Grand Ecore, and it was now certain that the fleet could not pass the falls at Alexandria. Lieuten-ant-Commander Selfridge, left in command of the fleet by the admiral, who had gone to Alexandria, addressed to me a dispatch, dated 17th of April, stating that he had been informed the army was to withdraw immediately, and that it would be impossible in that case to get the gun-boats down the river. I informed him at once that the army had no intention of withdrawing from that position; that I had sent to New Orleans for troops, and by a special messenger to General Steele, urging his direct co-operation, and that until it was definitely ascertained that his assistance would fail us, and that my force would be insufficient to advance farther upon this line against the enemy, who appeared to be in full force, I should entertain no thought of a retrograde movement, and never if it left the navy in any danger. No such purpose was then entertained, and until I received information in reply to my dispatches it was my purpose to maintain my position. A copy of this letter is appended to this report.

April 21, 1864...Natchitoches
Report of U.S. General A. J. Smith

On the morning of the 21st, I left Natchitoches and fell in the rear of the land column, which position I occupied with my command, alternating the divisions day by day until we reached Alexandria. From the day of our leaving Natchitoches, the enemy pushed the pursuit vigorously; the rear was skirmishing every day and nearly all day. Twice during the march we were obliged to form line and teach them a lesson.

April 22, 1864... Report of Maj.Gen. Banks:

The army moved on the morning of the 22d of April, every vessel having preceded both the marching orders and the movements of the army. Any statement from whatever source that the army contemplated moving from Grand Ecore toward Alexandria against the advance or without the approval of the naval officers in command, or until after the departure of every vessel on the river, is without the slightest color of truth. In my interview with Admiral Porter, on the 15th of April, he expressed the utmost confidence that the river would rise, and gave me no intimation of his leaving Grand Ecore, nor of the proposed withdrawal of his vessels, or of his apprehensions of the retreat of the army. I gave him at that time distinct information of my plans, which were to advance. This fact was communicated to Lt.-Com. Selfridge, in my letter of April 17. The admiral expressed the same confidence in the rise of the river to officers of the army, who from long experience in the Red River country were equally confident that it would not rise. The difficulties attending the voyage of the Eastport were incident to the condition of the river, for which the army was in no wise responsible. I had offered every assistance possible, and did not leave this position while any aid was suggested or required. Colonel Bailey, after consultation with the general officers of the army, offered to float the Eastport over the bars by the construction of wing-dams, similar to those afterward built at Alexandria, but the assistance was declined. No counsel from army officers was regarded in nautical affairs.

The army marched from Grand Ecore on the morning of the 22d of April, having been detained there by the condition of the navy ten days, to prevent the occupation of Monett's Bluff, on Cane River, a strong position, commanding the only road leading across the river to Alexandria, or to prevent the concentration of the enemy's forces at that point. If it was in his possession it became necessary to accomplish the evacuation without his knowledge, and to prevent his strengthening the natural defenses of the position by the rapidity of our march. The conflagration of a portion of the town at the hour appointed for marching partially frustrated the first object, but the second was fully accomplished.

Red River Campaign war ships

USS Eastport

USS Lexington

USS Benton

USS Lafayette, ironclad gunboat and ram, built 1848

USS Pittsburg, Commissioned 1862.

Porter's fleet consisted of 22 gun-boats, together with several supply steamers, hospital-boats, etc: including: Fort Herman, 7 guns ; Cricket, 8 guns ; Lafayette, 9 guns ; Neosho, 3 guns : Oscark, 2 guns ; Eastport, 9 guns ; Choctaw, 8 guns ; Osage, 3 guns; Chillicothe, 4 guns ; Louisville, 14 guns; Carondelet, 14 guns; Benton, 18 guns ; Pittsburg, 14 guns ; Gazette, 8 guns ; Mound City, 14 guns ; General Price, 4 guns; Lexington, 8 guns ; Ouachita, 3 guns ; Black Hawk, 13 guns.

April 23, 1864…

Report of U.S. Major General Nathaniel Banks:

The army marched from Grand Ecore to Cane River on the 20th [22d?] of April, a distance of 40 miles, and moved upon the position held by the enemy the 23d of April before daybreak. About 8,000 men and sixteen guns, under command of General Bee, were found in possession of the bluff on the opposite side of the river, who were evidently surprised at the unexpected presence of our army, but ready to dispute our only passage toward Alexandria. At daybreak one division of the Nineteenth and Thirteenth Corps each, the cavalry commanded by General Arnold, and the artillery commanded by Captain Closson, the whole under command of General W. H. Emory, were ordered forward to the river for the purpose of forcing this position. The pickets of the enemy were encountered on the west side of the river and quickly driven across, but the main position was found to be too strong to be carried by direct attack.

A reconnoitering party, under Colonel Bailey, Fourth Wisconsin Volunteers, sent to ascertain the practicability of crossing the river below the ferry toward Red River, on the morning of the 23d reported that the river was not fordable below the ferry, and that, owing to the impassable swamps on one side and the high bluffs on the other, it would not be possible to cross Cane River at any point below the ferry. If we failed to dislodge the enemy at the ferry the only alternative open to us was to attempt a crossing to the north side of Red River, an exceedingly difficult and dangerous movement. At the same time a force, under command of General H. W. Birge, consisting of his own command, the Third Brigade of the First Division, Nineteenth Army Corps, Colonel Fessenden commanding, and General Cameron's division, Thirteenth Corps, were ordered to cross the river 3 miles above the ferry, and, turning the left flank of the enemy, carry the heights in reverse if possible. Upon the successes of this movement depended the passage of the river by the army. The route traveled by General Birge's command was intersected by bayous, swamps, and almost impenetrable woods. This force reached its position late in the afternoon. To accomplish the purpose in view it became necessary to carry two strong positions held by pickets and skirmishers before the enemy was encountered in force on the crest of a hill, commanding an open field, over which our troops were compelled to cross in making the attack. The Third Brigade [First Division], Nineteenth Corps, Colonel Fessenden commanding, carried this position, which was defended with vigor, by assault. Its occupation compelled the retreat of the enemy from the bluffs commanding the ferry and ford. Our loss in this most brilliant and successful affair was about 200 killed and wounded. Colonel Fessenden, who led his command with great gallantry, was severely wounded.

General Birge, as in all actions in which he has been engaged, deserved and received the highest commendation. Lieut. William S. Beebe, of the ordnance department, and Mr. Young, of the engineer department, both volunteers, were conspicuous in the fight. Mr. Young was twice wounded, and died in New Orleans in July of the injuries received in this battle.

The attack on the rear of the enemy's position, covering the line of the enemy's retreat, failed in consequence of the difficulties encountered in the march and the late hour at which our troops gained their position. The enemy was thus enabled to escape with his artillery by the Fort Jesup road to Texas. The main body of the army had moved from Cloutierville at 4.30 a.m. on the 23d to the river. They drove in the enemy's pickets 3 miles in advance of the river, and formed a line of battle in front of the enemy's position, while General Birge was moving upon the enemy's left flank. The enemy opened with a heavy cannonade from his batteries, which was returned by our artillery with spirit and effect. The fire was continued at intervals during the morning, but the troops were held in reserve for the purpose of forcing the passage of the river at the moment that General Birge commenced his attack on the right. The action lasted till dark, when the enemy retreated and the heights were occupied by our forces. General A. J. Smith's command had sharp skirmishing with the advance of the enemy in our rear on the 23d. At 2 o'clock on the morning of the 24th, six guns were fired from the camp of the enemy in the rear. It was interpreted as a signal that they were ready for a combined attack, but the enemy in front had then been driven from the river and the contemplated movement upon our front and rear failed.

During the morning of the 23d, an effort had been made by a portion of the cavalry under Col. E. J. Davis to turn the right flank of the enemy's position by crossing the river below the ferry in the direction of Red River, which proved impracticable on account of impassable swamps. A sharp engagement occurred on the morning of the 24th, between the troops of General T. Kirby Smith and the enemy in the rear, which resulted in the repulse of the latter. Our loss was about 50 in this affair. Had the enemy concentrated his forces and fortified his position at Monett's Bluff we could not have forced him from it, and should have been compelled to accept the chances of crossing Red River above Cane River in the presence of the enemy on both sides of the river. Orders had been sent to General Grover to move with all his force upon Monett's Bluff, in the event of its being occupied by the enemy or our march seriously obstructed, and his troops were in readiness for this movement.

April 23, 1864...
Report of U.S. General A. J. Smith
At Cloutierville, on the 23d, they charged the rear division, General T. Kirby Smith's, but he repulsed them neatly and thoroughly after about an hour's fighting. During this engagement in the rear, the advance, having reached Cane River, found the bluffs on the other side occupied by a small force of the enemy, who disputed the crossing. Although the cavalry, Thirteenth, and Nineteenth Corps, were in advance of me, and notwithstanding the engagement with the enemy's cavalry in the rear, General Banks sent back an order for me to send General Mower with a strong brigade to force the passage of Cane River. Fearing to weaken my line during the engagement, I answered him in substance that it would be impracticable for me to comply with the order. Later in the day the passage was easily forced by detachments of the Thirteenth and Nineteenth Corps. On the afternoon of the

26th, we reached Alexandria and went into camp in line of battle, the Nineteenth Corps on the right, the Thirteenth Corps in advance of the center, and my command on the left. We remained in the vicinity of Alexandria in the same relative position until the 13th of May, the interim being occupied in getting the gun-boats over the falls and daily skirmishing with the enemy.

April 23, 1864...
Report of U.S. Major General Nathaniel Banks:
The army marched from Monett's Bluff on the afternoon of the 24th of April, and established lines of defense at Alexandria on the 25th and 26th April.

April, 1864...
Report of U.S. Major General Nathaniel Banks:

In the twenty-four days intervening between the departure of the army from Alexandria and its return the battles of Wilson's Farm, Sabine Cross-Roads, Pleasant Grove, Pleasant Hill, Campti, Monett's Bluff, and several combats in the neighborhood of Grand Ecore, while we were in occupation of that point, had been fought. In every one of these engagements, except that at Sabine Cross-Roads, we had been successful. The failure to accomplish the main object of the expedition was due to other considerations than the actual superiority of the enemy in the field. In these operations, in which my own command had marched by land nearly 400 miles, the total loss sustained was 3,980 men, of whom 289 were killed, 1,541 wounded, and 2,150 missing. A large portion of the latter were captured and have been since exchanged, but a considerable portion returned to the army during its operations on Red River. No loss of artillery or of trains or any army material whatever was sustained, except that which occurred at Sabine Cross-Roads. We lost there Nims' battery and a section of the Missouri Howitzer Battery, 150 wagons, and 800 mules, captured by the enemy on account of the position of the train near the field of battle. All the ammunition wagons were saved. The army had captured up to this time from the enemy 23 guns and 1,500 prisoners. His losses in killed, wounded, and prisoners, officers and men, were much greater than ours. Among the former were some of the most efficient rebel commanders, whose loss can never be made good. Up to this time no other loss of men or material had been sustained by our army. As soon as the lines of defense were completed preparations were made for the release of the fleet, which was then unable to pass below the falls. From the difficulty which the supply transports had encountered in passing the falls, it was known at Grand Ecore as early as the 15th of April that the navy could not go below, and the means for its release were freely discussed among officers of the army.

April 25, 1864...
Report of U.S. Major General Nathaniel Banks:

Upon my arrival at Alexandria, on the 25th of April, I found Major-General Hunter with dispatches from the lieutenant-general commanding the armies, reaffirming instructions which I had received at Grand Ecore relating to the operations of the army elsewhere, and to the necessity of bringing the Shreveport campaign to an end without delay. The only possible means of executing these peremptory orders had already been taken. General Hunter left on the 30th April, with dispatches to the lieutenant-general, giving a report of the condition of affairs; that the fleet could not pass the rapids; that there was no course for the army but to remain for its protection; that the enemy would concentrate all his forces at that point for the destruction of the army and the fleet, and that it was necessary to concentrate our troops west of the Mississippi at the same point by which the army and navy could be relieved and the forces of the enemy destroyed. Major-General McClernand, with the larger part of the forces recently at Matagorda Bay, which had been evacuated by order of Lieutenant-General Grant, dated March 31, arrived at Alexandria on the evening of the 29th of April. Brig. Gen. Fitz Henry Warren, left in command at Matagorda Bay, followed with the rest of the forces in Texas, except those on the Rio Grande, when the batteries of the enemy on the river near Marksville obstructed his passage. Not having sufficient force to dislodge the enemy, he seized Fort De Russy below the batteries, which he held until the passage of the fleet and army.

While engaged in the construction of the dam a dispatch was received from Major-General Halleck, dated April 30, as follows:

Lieutenant-General Grant directs that orders heretofore given be so modified that no troops be withdrawn from operations against Shreveport and on Red River, and that operations there be continued under the officer in command until further orders.

This dispatch was not received until it was impossible to move either up or down the river from Alexandria. It was, of course, impracticable to execute these instructions.

April 27, 1864
USS Covington lost on Red River

The USS Covington, sunk in Egg Bend on Red River.

　　The Covington had been ordered to report to Alexandria, Louisiana on 27 April 1864, Covington sailed with Signal protecting the Army transport Warner down the Red River.
　　At Egg Bend between Alexandria and Fort DeRussy, they were attacked by Confederate infantry in force. After five hours of bitter fighting, the transport was captured and the two escorts (Covington and Signal) were so badly damaged that they had to be abandoned and set afire. After Covington was set on fire by her crew, Lieutenant Lord and 32 of Covington's crew escaped to Alexandria.
　　Signal, however, was not so fortunate. After setting the ship on fire, her crew was captured by Confederate forces and made prisoners-of-war.

April 28, 1864
Report of U.S. General A. J. Smith

On the 28th of April, the enemy having driven in the skirmishers of the Thirteenth Corps, the corps fell back reluctantly, in compliance, it was said, with orders from Major-General Banks, three times repeated, abandoning and setting on fire their camp and garrison equipage, stores, and forage. Not knowing that it was done by order, I took the Second Brigade, Third Division, Sixteenth Army Corps, Col. William T. Shaw commanding, and put out the fire, rescued the stores, and saved much of the camp and garrison equipage. This brigade remained on the ground until the next morning, when it returned to its camp.

U. S. Major Gen. Nathaniel Banks   U. S. Gen. William B. Franklin

May 5, 1864
Loss of gunboats at Egg Bend, Avoyelles, Louisiana.

The community Egg Bend in Avoyelles Parish got its name from the bend of the Red River which came closest to the French community of the "Isle" or Island.

Similar to the bend of the river at Marksville which was the site for Fort DeRussy, Confederate authorities set up a position of cannons to guard the river at Egg Bend, between Choctaw Bayou in Fifth Ward and Dunn's Bayou at Echo.

When two U. S. Warships were separated from the rest of their fleet until Bailey's Dam was constructed, they were attacked, along with a civilian ship they were escorting at Egg Bend.

All three ships were lost, and this author was told by a resident in 1972 that remains could be seen of some them during low water. According to Steve Mayeux, the water was so low in the 1940s, that some local farmers were able to retrieve boards off at least one of the boats to use to repair barns. Mayeux also says that eight of the Union soldiers on board received National Medal of Honor, the highest award in the service for helping save some of the crew.

When the Red River was navigated in the 1970s, the sites were no longer identifiable nor assessable.

May 5th. 1864...Dunn's Bayou

Two scenes of the destruction of U.S. Transport John Warner by Confederate Batteries at Egg Bend on Red River, May 4. Cannons were set up on the south side of the river between Choctaw and Dunn Bayous. The top scene was in Harper's Illustrated Weekly.

U.S.S. Covington seen as it was destroyed at Egg Bend in Avoyelles.

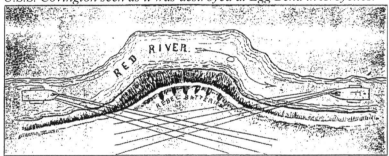

Map clearly shows the bend at Egg Bend, Louisiana, between Choctaw and Dunn Bayou.

Construction of Bailey's Dam

April 29 - May 9, 1864...River Dam
Report of Lt. Col. Uri Pearsall, 99th U.S. Colored Troops.

To Maj. GEORGE B. DRAKE, Assistant Adjutant-General.

In compliance with the request of the major-general commanding the department, I have the honor to submit the following report concerning the construction of the dam across Red River in the month of May last. I was in command of the Ninety-ninth U.S. Colored Infantry (formerly the Fifth Engineers, Corps d'Afrique) during the whole of the Red River campaign, my regiment forming a part of the engineer troops commanded by Col. George D. Robinson.

On the 29th of April this force was ordered to report to Lieut. Col. Joseph Bailey, then acting engineer Nineteenth Army Corps, for the purpose of constructing the dam above referred to. At the request of Colonel Bailey, Colonel Robinson and myself accompanied him to select the place for building the dam. After a thorough examination of the falls, Colonel Robinson and myself were of the opinion that two dams were necessary--one at the foot of the upper and the other at the foot of the lower falls. Colonel Bailey, however, decided that one would be sufficient, and accordingly we jointly selected the point at which the main dam was located.

On the morning of the 30th of April the troops selected for this duty were moved to convenient points near the dam and the work began at once. The force on the right bank consisted of the Ninety-seventh and Ninety-ninth U.S. Colored Infantry, under command of Col. George D. Robinson, of the former regiment, and a detail of 400 men from the brigade of colored infantry, commanded by Colonel Dickey. On the left bank were the Twenty-ninth Maine, portions of One hundred and tenth and One hundred and sixty-first New York Volunteers, and the pioneer corps of the Thirteenth Army Corps. Of the work on the left bank I know but little, my duties confining me exclusively to the right bank. At the commencement Lieutenant-Colonel Bailey placed me in charge of all the work on the right bank, which included the placing and the loading of the barges in the center of the river, together with the building of the "crib-dam" to the right bank. Colonel Robinson was designated by Colonel Bailey to procure necessary materials (for this purpose retaining the Ninety-seventh U.S. Colored Infantry), as also all necessary teams employed at this point. The remainder of the working forces were under my control.

The work progressed rapidly, as both officers and men became more confident of success than they were at the commencement, and on the afternoon of the 8th of May the channel was closed, with the exception of the three spaces of 20 feet each between the barges and a current of water under the second barge from the right bank, which was only partly loaded, it being our intention to merely scuttle it and place a sufficient amount of railroad iron on the top to prevent its rising up. Large braces were set diagonally up stream from the barges on each side, which, with large hawsers, were to prevent its being swept away, but the water rising rapidly, the weight proved insufficient for the purpose, and on the morning of the 9th it broke away, carrying with it the loaded barge nearest the right bank, both swinging in below and on the left-hand side of the new chute thus formed. This accident was in my opinion the most fortunate occurrence that could have taken place, those barges which were swept away serving to lengthen the chute and confine the volume of water passing through between them and the right bank, thus creating an artificial depth of water for the boats until they were fully below the ledge of rocks. They also answered as a "fender" to the boats and prevented their turning in passing through. The water was actually higher on the main dam when this took place than at any time afterward, and the navy, although not moving a single vessel until after the break occurred, were enabled to pass the gun-boats Lexington and Fort Hindman, also the light-draught monitors Neosho and Osage, over the falls above into the pond, and thence through the dam below in perfect safety.

At 7 o'clock on the morning of the 9th, Colonel Bailey directed me to leave a reliable officer in charge of tightening and repairing the remaining portion of the dam extending from the right bank, and then report to him in person on the same side of the river near the head of the falls, at which point he had decided to increase the depth of water by means of light wing-dams thrown out from each side. The forces moved from the lower or main dam consisted of detachments from the various regiments and the pioneer corps of Thirteenth Army Corps. The new plan was commenced with commendable vigor, the troops being employed in constructing the same as originally proposed until the afternoon of the 10th, which completed a temporary obstruction, close to each side of the channel, by means of light log cribs lashed together with rope and filled with brush and bricks. This work raised about 14 inches of water.

I will here state that in the mean time the gun-boat Chillicothe had managed to work her way through. The Carondelet attempted to follow, but owing to the rapidity of the current, and also to the wing-dams not being placed perpendicular to the direction of the channel, she was forced aside and lay with her bow close below the end of the wing-dam extending from the left bank, her stern being down stream and pointing diagonally across the channel. Several attempts were made to haul her from this position, all of which failed, and the navy finally concluded her case a hopeless one and thought there was sufficient room alongside for the others to pass. The Mound City was accordingly ordered to try it, and grounded abreast of the Carondelet. Five more iron-clads Were still above them.

Such, in brief, was the position of affairs on the afternoon of the 10th of May, as Major-General Banks will doubtless remember having a conversation with Colonel Bailey and myself at that time. It was at this crisis that Colonel Bailey asked me what could be done to relieve the boats. I replied in these words: "If you will allow me to build a dam where I please, on my own plan, and give me the men and materials I require, I will agree to put a foot of water under those boats (referring to the Mound City and Carondelet) by to-morrow night." He asked me what I required, and I told him the pioneer corps of the Thirteenth Army Corps to report to me at midnight to cross to the left bank, and that 10,000 feet of 2-inch plank should be there at 9 o'clock the next morning. Colonel Bailey agreed to this proposition, and accordingly about 1 a.m. of that night Captain Hutchens, commanding the pioneers, reported to me for duty. Immediate steps were taken to get across the river. I hailed every boat in the fleet to obtain cutters for this purpose, but the reply of all was, "wait until daylight." We were accordingly forced to do so, and it was sunrise before all were across to the opposite side. I immediately instructed the men in building two-legged trestles for a "bracket dam." They worked with even greater energy than ever before, and the trestles were all made by 9 a.m. Some pieces of iron bolts (size one-half inch) were procured and one set into the foot of the legs of each trestle; also one in the cap pieces at the end resting on the bottom, up stream. The place selected by me for this "bracket dam" was at a point opposite the lower end of the Carondelet, extending out close to this vessel from the left bank. A party of men, selected and headed by myself, placed these trestles in position there under very adverse circumstances, the water being about 4 feet deep and very swift, and coupled with a very slippery bottom, making it almost impossible to stand against the current. Several men were swept away in this duty, but no lives were lost. The trestles were fastened as soon as they were in position by means of taking "sets" and driving the iron bolts above referred to down into the bottom. All were in position by 10 a.m., and the plank having arrived all that remained was to place them. This was done in less than an hour, and by 11 a.m. there was at least a foot of water thrown under the Mound City and the Carondelet and both vessels floated off easily before the ultimate height of water was obtained. The five remaining vessels passed with but little difficulty, and at noon on the following day were safe below the main dam at Alexandria.

Much has been said of the part taken by the navy in rescuing their fleet, and I deem it proper to state my honest convictions. To Captain Langthorne, of the Mound City, and

Admiral Porters fleet above Alexandria on Red River

USS Black Hawk, gunboat

the officers and men employed with him, great praise is due. In regard to any other efforts put forth by them I must say that none other were observed by me, and it seems incredible that much could have been done by them in my absence. I slept but twenty-nine hours during those twelve eventful days. My meals were almost invariably brought to me; therefore my presence was almost constant.

It may be said that the navy loaned ropes, made bolts, etc., but in so doing they performed the duties of the quartermaster's department only while on the other hand, there is much in this report showing that they caused a delay of six hours at the most critical point of our operations, whereas if no delay had occurred in the building of the bracket dam that saved seven of their best iron-clads, the army could have moved a day sooner from Alexandria. These facts can be substantiated by many officers besides myself, and the impartial historian will [not], neither could, with propriety make any other record than that the army of General Banks saved the fleet of Admiral Porter.

In conclusion, I would beg leave to state that the project of building a dam across Red River, although difficult, could never have been pronounced impracticable by any men who followed a similar avocation in civil life. The bottom and shores being so extremely favorable, and official reports having been promulgated by the naval authorities asserting that Colonel Bailey was the only man in the army who believed the plan practicable, that he was the originator of it.

I deem it my duty to refute assertions so far as they concern myself, having waited three months to see it contradicted by others. The major-general will recollect of my assurances to him in this respect ere the work had fairly begun. It can also be proved that it was pronounced feasible by me while at Grand Ecore. These statements are made in self-defense, without doubting that the credit justly belongs to others; yet were such statements substantiated against an officer like myself, after ten years of practical experience in building dams on the most difficult rivers in the country, it would be deemed sufficient evidence by me of my utter incompetency to hold my present position.

I have the honor to be your obedient servant,
U. B. PEARSALL, Lieut Col. 99th U.S. Colored Infantry.

May 4, 1864

Governor Moore's Plantation, Rapides
HDQRS. FIRST AND THIRD DIVS., 16TH ARMY CORPS, Moore's Plantation, May 4, 1864.

GENERAL: A negro just escaped from the rebels states that they are in large force in our front; says. he heard their drums beating this morning, which shows conclusively that they have infantry. I tried to develop their forces yesterday, but did not succeed, and I also attempted the same this morning, but failed. I do not deem it prudent to risk an engagement with a bayou in my rear. I have therefore taken a position north of the bayou, near Governor Moore's residence. Had I had cavalry, I could have ascertained the strength of the enemy without bringing on a general engagement. The negro from whom I have obtained the above information states that he heard the rebels in their conversation with one and another talk boastingly of having 30,000 men. This is undoubtedly an exaggeration, yet I think it evident that they are largely superior to the force under my command.

    I am, general, very respectfully, your obedient servant,
        JOS. A. MOWER, Brigadier- General, Commanding.
    - Official Records of the War of the Rebellion Series

May 8, 1864

Chamber's Plantation, Rapides (Present site of LSU-A)
    Houston Daily Telegraph Friday, May 27, 1864
    Headquarters 1st Cavalry Div., Army West La., May 8, 1864
General Order: The Brig. Gen. commanding takes occasion to call The attention of their comrades to the gallantry displayed by the officers and men of Terrell's and Likens' regiments in the engagement with the enemy on the 2d inst., at the Chambers' plantation, in charging his largely superior force of cavalry and infantry, strongly posted in the negro quarters on the plantation, and behind a fence running east of the trench, against five fold odds they charged with a yell, led on by Col. Terrell driving the enemy in confusion, at sunset from their position: The example of those men should excite the emulation of the army to renewed efforts to drive from the land the enemy who now attempts to waste by fire a country he has been unable to conquer by the sword.
        By command of Brig. Gen. A.P. BAGBY,
    J. P. Smith, A.A.G. Commanding Division.
Transcribed by William J. Bozic, Jr. on June 17, 2009 from microfilm copy of the original newspaper held in the City of Houston (Texas) Public Library's Julia Ideson Building.

Union boats escape low water of Red River at Alexandria thanks to Bailey's Dam

May 8-9, 1864

Report of Lieut. Col. Joseph Bailey, 4th Wisconsin Cavalry, Engineer Officer 19th Army Corps. to Maj. W. Hoffman:

MAJOR: I have the honor to make the following report in reference to the construction of the dam across Red River, at the foot of the Alexandria falls, for the purpose of releasing that portion of Admiral Porter's Mississippi Squadron which was unable to pass the falls, owing to the low stage of the water. Immediately after our army received a check at Sabine Cross-Roads and the retreat commenced I learned through reliable sources that the Red River was rapidly falling. I became assured that by the time the fleet could reach Alexandria there would not be sufficient water to float the gun-boats over the falls. It was evident, therefore, that they were in imminent danger. Believing, as I did, that their capture or destruction would involve the destruction of our army, the blockade of the Mississippi, and even greater disasters to our cause, I proposed to Major-General Franklin on the 9th of April, previous to the battle of Pleasant Hill, to increase the depth of water by means of a dam, and submitted to him my plan of the same. In the course of the conversation he expressed a favorable opinion of it.

During the halt of the army at Grand Ecore on the 17th of April, General Franklin, having heard that the iron-clad gun-boat East-port had struck a snag on the preceding day and sunk at a point 9 miles below, gave me a letter of introduction to Admiral Porter and directed me to do all in my power to assist in raising the Eastport, and to communicate to the admiral my plan of constructing a dam to relieve the fleet, with his belief in its practicability; also that he thought it advisable that the admiral should at once confer with General Banks and urge him to make the necessary preparations, send for tools, etc. Nothing further was done until after our arrival at Alexandria. On the 26th, the admiral reached the head of the falls. I examined the river and submitted additional details of the proposed dam. General Franklin approved of them and directed me to see the admiral and again urge upon him the necessity of prevailing upon General Banks to order the work to be commenced immediately. There was no doubt that the entire fleet then above the rapids would be lost unless the plan of raising the water by a dam was adopted and put into execution with all possible vigor. I represented that General Franklin had full confidence in the success of the undertaking, and that the admiral might rely upon him for all the assistance in his power. The only preliminary required was an order from General Banks. On the 29th, by order of General Franklin, I consulted with Generals Banks and Hunter, and explained to them the proposed plan in detail. The latter remarked that, although he had little confidence in its feasibility, he nevertheless thought it better to try the experiment, especially as General Franklin, who is an engineer, advised it. Upon this General Banks issued the necessary order for details, teams, etc., and I commenced the work on the morning of the 30th.

I presume it is sufficient in this report to say that the dam was constructed entirely on the plan first given to General Franklin, and approved by him.

During the first few days I had some difficulty in procuring details, etc., but the officers and men soon gained confidence and labored faithfully. The work progressed rapidly, without accident or interruption, except the breaking away of two coal barges which formed part of the dam. This afterward proved beneficial. In addition to the dam at the foot of the falls, I constructed two wing-dams on each side of the river at the head of the falls.

The width of the river at the point where the dam was built is 758 feet, and the depth of the water from 4 to 6 feet. The current is very rapid, running about 10 miles per hour. The increase of depth by the main dam was 5 feet 4 inches; by the wing-dams, 1 foot 2 inches; total, 6 feet 6 inches. On the completion of the dam, we had the gratification of seeing the entire fleet pass over the rapids to a place of safety below, and we found ample reward for our labors in witnessing their result. The army and navy were relieved from a painful suspense, and eight valuable gun-boats saved from destruction. The cheers of the masses assembled on the shore when the boats passed down attested their joy and renewed confidence. To Major-General Franklin, who, previous to the commencement of the work, was the only supporter of my proposition to save the fleet by means of a dam, and whose persevering efforts caused its adoption, I desire to return my grateful thanks. I trust the country will join with the Army of the Gulf and the Mississippi Squadron in awarding to him due praise for his earnest and intelligent efforts in their behalf. Major-General Banks promptly issued all necessary orders and assisted me by his constant presence and co-operation. General Dwight, his chief of staff, Colonel Wilson and Lieutenant Sargent, aides-de-camp, also rendered valuable assistance by their personal attention to our wants. Admiral Porter furnished a detail from his ships' crews, under command of an excellent officer, Captain Langthorne, of the Mound City. All his officers and men were constantly present, and to their extraordinary exertions and to the well-known energy and ability of the admiral much of the success of the undertaking is due. I am also under many obligations to

Major Sentell, provost-marshal, and Lieutenant Williamson, ordnance officer, of General Franklin's staff; to Lieut. Col. W. B. Kinsey, One hundred and sixty-first New York Volunteers; to Lieut. Col. U. B. Pearsall, Ninety-ninth U.S. Colored Infantry, who was my assistant; to Capt. George W. Stein, Sixteenth Ohio, and to Captains Harding, Morrison, and Harper, of the Ninety-ninth U.S. Colored Infantry, all of whom exhibited much practical knowledge and untiring zeal.

The following is a list of the troops who constructed the dam: Pioneer corps of the Thirteenth Army Corps, under Captain Hutchens, Twenty-fourth Indiana Volunteers, Lieutenant Smout, Twenty-third Wisconsin Volunteers, and Lieutenant Kimbley, Twenty-fourth Indiana Volunteers; Twenty-ninth Maine Volunteers, Lieutenant-Colonel Emerson; Ninety-ninth U.S. Colored Infantry, Lieutenant-Colonel Pearsall; Ninety-seventh U.S. Colored Infantry, Col. G. D. Robinson; and detachments from the Twenty-third and Twenty-ninth Wisconsin Volunteers, Twenty-seventh Indiana Volunteers, Nineteenth Kentucky Volunteers, Sixteenth and Twenty-third Ohio Volunteers, Twenty-fourth Iowa Volunteers, Seventy-seventh and One hundred and thirtieth Illinois Volunteers, and from other regiments. These details labored patiently and enthusiastically by day and night, standing waist deep in the water, under a broiling sun. Their reward is the consciousness of having performed their duty as true soldiers, and they deserve the gratitude of their countrymen.

I have the honor to be, your obedient servant,
J. BAILEY,
Lieut. Cot. and Actg..Mil. Eng. 19th Army Corps

Alexandria, as seen during the war before it was burned in May.

As the Union Army floated down Red River through Bailey's Dam, soldiers set the town afire. The pastor of the Catholic Church stood on the steps of the building and convinced the Yankees to spare his church building..It was the only building left standing downtown after their departure. This image is in the museum at Fort Buhlow in Pineville, LA.

May 11, 1864 *Gen. Bee honored*
Houston Daily Telegraph
Wednesday June 8, 1864 No 288 p.1 c. 5
(Transcribed by William J. Bozic, Jr. Dec 16, 2008.)

Marksville, La.
May 11, 1864

The undersigned officers of the 1st division, being in active campaign, and without facilities of assembling together, beg leave to present individually to Gen H. P. Bee, an assurance of our high appreciation of his conduct while in command of this Division.

From the month of November, 1863, to the present time, he has commanded this division; he has led it on many battle fields, and has ever been distinguished for his gallantry and cool indifference to danger, whilest exercising a wise caution and prudence, which enabled this small command to keep in check the movements of a largely superior force of the enemy, all the time annoying and harassing them.

We believe that the division has rendered material service to the country and cause, and that, with the aid of that experience which every day's contact with the enemy gave, Gen. Bee's future as a commander was fraught with promise to the cause, and honor of himself. We beg to tender expressions of regret which we all feel in parting with him, and our best wishes for his future success and happiness.

Very respectfully, &c.

J.B. Likens, Col. Com'dg. 35th Texas Cavalry
J.R. Burns, Lieut. Col.   "   "   "
J.O. Robertson, Lieut. Col. com'dg. Terrell's Regt. Cavalry

Wm. O. Yager, Col. com'dg 1st Texas Cav.
A.W. Terrell, Col com'dg 2d. Brig. Div.

P.C. Woods, Col. com'dg 32^{d} Texas Cavalry
W.O. Hutchinson, Major   "   "   "
H.C. Gould, Col. com'dg 23d Texas Cav
Wm. G. Vincent, Col. com'dg 2d Regt. La.

May 11-15, 1864

Marksville-Cocoville

The early days in May leading up to the Battle of Mansura are described by Felix Poche:

Wednesday May 11. Our division began to march toward Marksville, and is camped several miles from there. The enemy is bombarding our Batteries on Red River with their gun boats.

Thursday May 12. Today we reached Cocoville where we are camped. T

Friday May 13. We are camped at Cocoville....At the invitation of my good friend Philogene Coco I had dinner today at Mr. A. D. Coco's, in company with several officers of the 18th [Louisiana] Regt. The enemy, with the gunboat Choctaw, bombarded our pickets on the river all day and killed one of our men from Polignac's Division. It is reported that the enemy descends the river today.

Saturday May 14. Our Brigade began its march today, and traveling by Mansura we covered 10 miles and camped on the Evergreen Road. We heard heavy cannonading on the river. It is said the enemy is advancing."

*May 15, Cavalry Skirmish near Marksville & Cocoville
Sunday May 15. We remained in camp all day, and heard a heavy cannonade in the direction of the Red River. The enemy is advancing on the prairie, and had had quite a skirmish with our cavalry, near Marksville and Cocoville.*

At sunset our division started to march in battle formation at the border of the woods along the edge of the Mansura Prairie. In that position and with every appearance of an engagement tomorrow, we slept on the ground and I slept very well all night.

May 12, 1864

History of 5th Vol., (Pelican artillery) of St. James Parish:
On May 12, four guns of the Pelican artillery fired on a Federal tinclad gunboat on the Red River near Mrs. DAVID's Plantation, driving the vessel away. The battery participated in the engagements at Marksville, May 15; Mansura, May 16; Moreauville, May 17; and Yellow Bayou, May 18.

May 13, 1864

Report of U.S. General A. J. Smith
On the 13th of May, the boats having passed the falls, the retreat was again resumed, my command falling into its old place in the rear. Continuing down the river as far as Fort DeRussy, in order to be at hand to protect the boats if necessary, we reached the fort on the night of the 14th. From this point the guards on the boats were considered sufficient to protect them, and they were therefore ordered around to Simmesport, on the Atchafalaya Bayou, toward which the land column was turned. On the 15th instant, while crossing Avoyelles Prairie, a brigade of the enemy's cavalry, with about twelve pieces of artillery, appeared in front and attempted to delay and annoy the column. My command was ordered forward into line on the right of the Nineteenth Corps, the Thirteenth Corps being on the extreme left. Line being formed, I sent Capt. William S. Burns, acting assistant inspector-general of my staff, to report the fact and ask for instructions, which were given him by Brig. Gen. William Dwight, chief of staff of Major-General Banks, in the following words: "Say to General Smith that the Thirteenth Corps will press their (the enemy's) right. He with his command will attack their left, while with the Nineteenth Corps we pierce their center."

As the several commands moved forward in line to execute these instructions, the brigade of cavalry galloped away, taking their artillery with them.

May 14, 1864 Battle of Mansura
Report of U.S. Major General Nathaniel Banks:

The army on its march from Alexandria did not encounter the enemy in force until near the town of Mansura. He was driven through the town in the evening of the 14th [?] of May, and at daybreak next morning our advance encountered his cavalry on the prairie east of the town. He fell back with steady and sharp skirmishing across the prairie to a belt of woods, which he occupied. The enemy's position covered three roads diverging from Mansura to the Atchafalaya. He manifested a determination here to obstinately resist our passage. The engagement, which lasted several hours, was confined chiefly to the artillery until our troops got possession of the edge of the woods, first upon our left by General Emory, and subsequently on our right by General Smith, when he was driven from the field, after a sharp and decisive fight, with considerable loss.

Steve Mayeux, historian on Battle of Mansura:

The Battle of Mansura has generally been described, by a lot of the participants, as one of the most glorious battles of the entire war, in that the whole battle line, several miles long, was viewable by everyone there, and there were lots of flags and gleaming bayonets and cannons shooting and horses snorting . . . and almost no one got hurt. More animal casualties than human. There were a few killed and wounded, but as Civil War battles went, very few.

The battle was very fluid, and the lines moved constantly - picture the Yankees coming down from Marksville, stretched from Old Hwy 1 about two miles toward Hessmer, moving toward Mansura. The Confederates held Mansura at the start of the battle, and gradually fell back, eventually side-stepping out of the Union's way toward Hessmer, and letting the Yanks move on to Moreauville and eventually, Simmesport.

I've only found two dead Yankees by name, with 40-50 wounded, mostly minor wounds. The Confederates had a few more dead, but not many. After the battle, the Yankees moved toward the Atchafalaya, with the rear guard sleeping in Moreauville that night. The Confederates came in behind them after they passed.

1st Lt. Co." I " John J Moncure of Terrell's Regiment on May 15th:

.... I witness(ed) his (Col. Terrell) gallant conduct on the 15th, while covering our retreat at Marksville, where he commanded his brigade and obstinately contested every inch of ground with the enemy from 11o'clock AM, until it was too dark to see, during which he evinced more courage and coolness than I have ever witnessed, keeping himself frequently in an exposed condition between his man in the enemy, and moving with his usual restless energy to every part of the battlefield, where his presence might be needed, and after the firing ceased, he was so completely exhausted, he could scarcely sit on his horse. *(Transcribed by William J. Bozic, Jr. Houston, Texas June 23, 2012. All Rights Reserved.)*

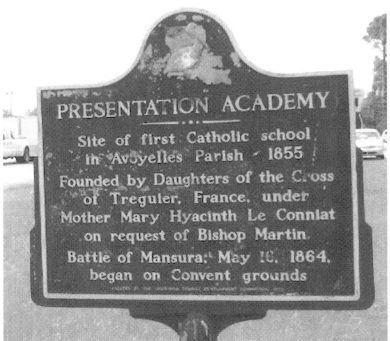

Marker notes Battle of Mansura began in Cocoville. on Convent grounds.

Cocoville Engagement described by Catholic Nun in Avoyelles, Sister Hyacinth

 A group of nuns came from France before the war where they established a Catholic school in Cocoville between Mansura and Marksville..

The Mother Superior, Mary Hyainth Le Conniat, wrote in a letter about the battle as it began in Cocoville near the Convent and made its way to Mansura: *Pentecost Sunday, they came to tell me the enemy was three miles from us. You could see consternation painted on all faces. We hid our sacred vessels and the vestments. Then, I asked our Sis-ters to go into the woods with our boarders, who numbered forty to forty-five. Father Rebours and four of our Sisters stayed with me to guard the house. If ever I had been near death, that was the day. The Community was between two armies. A bomb* *exploded above our heads, and destroyed a wooden bed, and created much damage in the convent. Five bombs fell upon our little chapel, broke the statue of St. Joseph, etc. Our animals were enclosed in a little field near the chapel. A bullet killed four: a cow, a heifer, and two sheep. More than fifty cannon balls and I do not know how many bullets crossed over the Community for three hours, while the battle went on. God did not allow a single bullet to strike us! [The Sisters took refuge in a large oven. Only a statue in the chapel received no damage.] As soon as the battle was over, about thirty of the Federals came to the Community, into the convent, think-ing no one was there. When they saw us, they exclaimed: "0, they are Sisters of Charity!" They asked us for a drink and then they left. . .. The Pastor, our Sisters, and the pupils came back at 9 o'clock at night. Our soldiers had retreated toward the bayou and the next day at 5 o'clock in the morning, the enemy was in the neighborhood again. Useless was it to ask for protection this time. They were irritated over their defeat. They were twice as many as our Con-federates in number. They revenged themselves upon the country—pillaging, looting, and burning! We were not spared! You know our fence is six feet high. It is made of wood, with no ditches nearby. All our fields are enclosed by a wooden fence. The enemy enjoyed tearing down the fences, burning them, and laying waste to everything. They had 1,500 wagons or carts with them. They came through our enclosure and garden with this train of carts. More than 100 of these brigands made a tour of our en-closure, our grounds. We had to tell them it was against the law for them to steal and destroy such an establishment as ours. They did not care. They took 100 barrels of corn from our storehouse, more than 150 of the poultry, all our animals (horned ones), thirty-six cows, and calves in all, a mule worth 1,500 francs, or $300 in gold to us. Happily, they did not find our sacred vessels and the church vestments. We have estimated the damage and loss at $1,500 or 7,500 francs. . . to our Community alone. We have made formal complaint, filing a suit, but I do not believe we will get anything, any response to our claim. There is no justice in this country. God will repay us bountifully, we hope, in Heaven.*

This large army was composed of about 30,000 or 40,000 troops—even when they were in retreat. From 6 o'clock in the morning until 2 o'clock in the afternoon the carts were passing, as well as the soldiers, horses, etc., in no set order whatsoever. It was something that was more than terrible. At 10 o'clock we had a guard. Without this protection, they would have taken even our clothes, etc. We succeeded in getting back only one cow and two heifers.

1st Lt. Co." I " John J Moncure of Terrell's Regiment wrote about May 16:

He (Col. Terrell) was with us again on the morning of the 16th, when his brigade supported, three of our batteries near Mansura and Cocoville, where for four hours we were exposed to the heaviest shelling, admitted by all, that had ever occurred this side of the Mississippi, where from fatigue and loss of sleep, he was forced to yield to exhausted nature, which he reluctantly did on advice of his surgeon after slowly riding the entire length of his line, and exhorting his men to again, as they had so frequently done, do their whole duty, as he was too unwell to command them during the remainder of the day. He then surrendered the command of his brigade to Col. Yeager, and his regiment to the gallant Lieut. Col. Robertson- than whom braver and more noble spirits do not exist.
(Transcribed-William Bozic, Jr. Houston, TX, 2012. All Rights Reserved.)

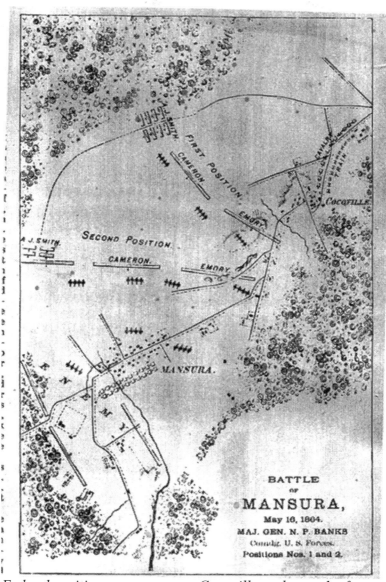

Federal positions are seen near Cocoville to the north of Mansura. Confederates lined up against Bayou Lacombe in downtown Mansura.

May 17 1864, Moreauville

The day after the battle of Mansura, the war went down what is today roughy the path of Louisiana state highway No. 1, through Moreauville towards the Atchafalaya. Union troops thwarted their rebels by destroying a bridge over Bayou des Glaises at Moreauville:

May 17, Battle of Moreauville, at the Burning Bridge:
Union soldier's report provided by Steve Mayeux, historian:

When it was ascertained that the enemy was in force in our rear, on the 17th, Companies B and F under command of Lieutenants Newhall and Beckford respectively, were ordered to remain on the north or west side of the bayou, holding a position on the top of a bluff, and to keep the enemy back while the rest of the troops crossed the bridge and got into position.

These orders were that when the bridge was well on fire, a signal would be given and then we were to cross. These orders were carried out. The enemy showed in force, but these two gallant little companies kept up a sharp fire, leading the rebs to think that we still had a large force that side of the bayou. By reason of the high bank at that place, they could not see the bayou. When the bridge was well blazing, we were ordered across. We withdrew a part of the men at a time and before the rebels. knew what we were up to, we were safely across, Lieutenants Beckford and Newhall bringing up the rear. In meantime the enemy has appeared across the bayou, and all along the bluff, yelling as only Johnnies could yell. Finding the bridge gone they moved a large force around the bayou to our left. The bayou here was almost in the shape of a horseshoe and our line, after the crossing just made, was formed about across the centre inside. Our orders were to hold this position until relieved or ordered back.

The enemy opened on us with a battery from the bluff, but fortunately fired over our heads. We soon saw that the rebs. had crossed the bayou on our left, and were coming up in our rear. Just at this time Lieutenant Beckford received a bad wound in the shoulder and was taken to the rear. Lieutenant Haskins, "Jud," had just told his men, Company A, to "sock it to 'em" when he caught a hot one in the side and had also to be taken from the field.

May 18, 1864, Yellow Bayou
Modern report by Steve Mayeux, historian:

This Civil War fort was established by Gen. Dick Taylor to protect the Atchafalaya River and other tributaries from the Union forces.

It was named "Old Oaks" by the Union forces, "Norwood Plantation Fort" by the local people and "Fort Humbug" by the soldiers who used it.

Historians later named the site **"Yellow Bayou Civil War Fort"**

It was defended by forces of Maj. Polignac, Maj. Wharton, Lt. Xavier Debray and Col. W. O. Yager of the Confederate Army under the command of Gen. Taylor. Attacking forces were commanded by Col. George Robinson, Gen. William Dwight, Gen Arnold, Major Mower, Capt. George Burmiester, and Col. Lucas, all under the command of Gen. A. J. Smith and Gen N. K. Banks, who was later demoted to private at Simmesport.

The battle for the fort began in the morning of May 18, 1864, and ended that same day when a brush fire started. The major battle began the following day and lasted only three hours and 40 minutes.

Over 18,000 Union soldiers were reportedly thrown against the 4,000 Confederate soldiers. There were 608 casualties among the Southern soldiers and 350 on the Union side.

Besides these, Gen. Burmiester was shot through the chest and Col. G. S. Hill was wounded in the ankle. Hill's son was shot in the head and killed.

Steve Mayeux, historian:

The Yankees Return

The abandonment of Fort Humbug in March marked the opening of the Red River Campaign. Two months later the fort would be involved again in the final days of the campaign. The Union attempt to enter Texas had been a failure, and on May 17, 1864, the lead elements of the whipped army of some 30,000 troops were being driven past

Fort Humbug by a Confederate army about one-fifth that size.

Yellow Bayou was defended by forces of Maj. Polignac, Maj. Wharton, Lt. Xavier Debray and Col. W. O. Yager of the Confederate Army under the command of Gen. Taylor.
Attacking forces were commanded by Col. George Robinson, Gen. William Dwight, Gen Arnold, Major Mower, Capt. George Burmiester, and Col. Lucas, all under the command of Gen. A. J. Smith and Gen N. K. Banks, who was later demoted to private at Simmesport.

Homer Sprague, of the 13th Connecticut, reported passing "some new and strong fortifications on Yellow Bayou, the principal of which was called Fort Lafayette. The rebels evacuated them at our approach." The 83rd Ohio Volunteer Infantry "followed Bayou LaGlaze adn crossed a small bayou at Fort taylor, which was being leveled by prisoneers." About noon on the 17th, the 114th New York State Volunteers "crossed Bayou Yellow upon a pontoon bridge, passing through some rebel works which were commenced a year before, with the intention of holding the road at the crossing. They were well planned, at an extensive scale, but the enemy being compelled to change his line of defense, they were abandoned unfinished."

Destruction of Fort Humbug
Colonel George D. Robinson, Commanding Engineer Brigade, had arrived at "Yellow Bush Bayou, 3 miles from Simsport," at 4 a.m. on May 17. By 6 a.m. he had a pontoon bridge ready to cross troops, and encamped his Third Engineers "on the east bank of Yellow Bush Bayou. On the west bank of the bayou the enemy had constructed two formidable earth-works, designed to prevent the advance of our army from Simsport. About noon, May 17, I received orders from General Emory to reverse these works and make a tete-de-pont of them, and on the following day received orders from him to destroy the works entirely." It was probably at this tome that the larger fort, at the junction of Yellow Bayou and Bayou des Glaises, adjacent to the pontoon bridge, was destroyed. The other fort, further to the south and

approximately 1 mile from the bridge, escaped destruction.

Fort Humbug in the Battle of Yellow Bayou

The battle for the fort began in the morning of May 18, 1864, and ended that same day when a brush fire started. The major battle began the following day and lasted only three hours and 40 minutes.

Over 18,000 Union soldiers were reportedly thrown against the 4,000 Confederate soldiers. There were 608 casualties among the Southern soldiers and 350 on the Union side.

Besides these, Gen. Burmiester was shot through the chest and Col. G. S. Hill was wounded in the ankle. Hill's son was shot in the head and killed.

At the beginning of the Battle of Yellow Bayou on May 18, 1864, the 33rd Missouri Infantry Volunteers received orders to move from "the rear of the levee on Avoyelles Bayou, and take a position in the center of the field, in front of Fort Carroll and on the left of Battery M, First Missouri Light Artillery." Arthur McCullough, of the 81st Illinois Infantry, mentions forming a line across the bayou from a fort while "a brisk fight took place across the bayou opposite us." There is also an article from the Galveston newspaper concerning the battle, presented as a third-hand account of the action, which maintains that "the main battle took place in and around the old works erected by our army last winter, the Federals occupying the fortifications." This varies so greatly from all other accounts that it lacks credibility. These are the only references to any Fort Humbug fortifications in any of the battle reports, official or unofficial, that the author has been able to locate. It is very unlikely that Fort Humbug was involved in the battle.

Various Names

There appears to have been no official name for Fort Humbug. The soldiers who built the fort referred to it as Fort Humbug. The Union troops who observed it referred to it (or to its component parts) variously as Fort Humbug, Fort Scurry, Fort Taylor, Fort Lafayette, Fort Morgan and Fort Carroll.

May 18, 1864
Report of U.S. General A. J. Smith

On the 18th of May, while lying in line protecting the crossing of the other corps, the enemy made a severe attack on the lines, driving in the skirmishers. I was at the time at the landing, but had left orders with General Mower, in case the enemy attacked, to use whatever force was necessary to drive them back. He therefore ordered the line forward, driving them easily for about 2 miles across an open field and through a briar thicket, thickly interspersed with dead trees on the other side, beyond which he found them drawn up in force far outnumbering his, with about twenty pieces of artillery posted to support them. Withdrawing to the edge of the first field General Mower formed line, concealed by the thicket, and bringing his artillery up to close range awaited their advance. They soon came, when, after giving them a few rounds of canister and case-shot, he ordered a charge with the bayonet, repulsing them with terrible slaughter and driving them again through the thicket into the field beyond under protection of their artillery.

Withdrawing to his old position near the thicket they charged him again, and were a second time driven back with severe loss. The firing during the second charge set the thicket on fire, so that it formed a barrier impassable for either party. Withdrawing his troops to the open field, General Mower sent those that had been the heaviest engaged to their camps and formed a new line with the remainder, who bivouacked in line during the night. We captured 156 prisoners in the charge. Our loss was: Killed, 38; wounded, 226; missing, 3; total, 267. Lists of casualties and captures are herewith inclosed, with reports of brigade and division commanders. No further attack was made, and pursuit by the enemy stopped from this day.

Descriptions of the Battle of Yellow Bayou:

Officer Felix Poche described the 18th at Yellow Bayou:

Thursday May 18. Battle of Yellow Bayou. Today at 10 o'clock our division received orders to march toward Simmesport, without wagons, only the ambulances and the ordnance wagons. Arriving at Norwood plantation we found our artillery and two Brigades of our cavalry actively engaged with the enemy.,,,

We were placed in Battle formation at the edge of the woods below the Norwood plantation house at the point where a large sugar cane field ends. A Cavalry Brigade was on the right wing of our line. Appearing on foot in the center was Mouton's [Gray's] Brigade (including the 18th), and as the left wing Polignac's [Stone's] Brigade.

Our sharpshooters were not very far in advance in the woods and soon began a steady exchange of fire with the enemy, whose line of battle slowly advanced, and after one-half hour of skirmishing the two lines began to open mutual fire, which was very strong and steady for nearly an hour. But the enemy amassed their infantry on our left wing and destroyed Polignac's [Stone's] Brigade and caused them to flee in disorder with a great loss including their commander Colonel Stone. Our left wing was without protection, the 28th [Louisiana] of our Brigade became disorderly, in view of which Genl Gray ordered his Brigade to retreat. I hastened to transmit the order to the Crescent [Regiment] of which only one part retreated, and arriving at the 18th [Louisiana] I saw that the Regiment had repulsed the enemy, with the help of the Brigade of Texas Cavalry and was in hot pursuit. After having rallied some of the stragglers I hastened to Gen' Gray to report to him the state of affairs, and asked him to have the other two Regiments advance, but he showed me that the enemy had completely destroyed our left wing, and were almost on the field.

He then sent me to search for the 18th [Louisiana], which I found far back in the Woods, having entirely repulsed the enemy and who were in perfect Battle formation awaiting orders. I transmitted the order to retreat to the valiant commander, Capt Sanchez, who brought the Regiment to the line occupied by the rest of the Brigade[.] On coming out of the Woods, the noble and heroic Regiment were received with cries of joy and of homage by the Texans, who gave three resounding hurrahs for the chivalrous 18th of Louisiana, who had so proudly and so courageously repulsed the enemy's Cavalry."

Our Artillery then opened its deadly fire on the enemy to our Left and immediately put them to flight, so that we were left masters of the Battlefield[.] Meanwhile nightfall was approaching and our troops having been in action for more than 3 hours and harassed by fatigue were quietly withdrawn from the field. The enemy's artillery was then placed in position and exchanged a few shots with ours, but this last duel lasted but a few minutes, and peace at last reigned over the bloody field of carnage.

Our Brigade lost in that battle 40 men, 31 wounded and 25 mis-sing. Polignac's [Stone's] [lost] 40, of which the greater part were wounded, and it is thought that losses in the cavalry amounted to something on the order of 300 men during the Battle of Yellow Bayou. Gen]. Wharton who commands our forces says that the enemy's losses are equal to ours. Our poor soldiers dead with fatigue and blinded with dust were marched to the camp on Bayou Black Water [L'eau Noir] four or five miles from the battlefield. One poor soldier of the Crescent Regiment was killed on the field by the accidental discharge of his gun which blew off half of his head.

Silas Grismore reported burials of both Confederates and Union soldiers. *More than fifty of our men were buried in one cemetery near a brick church, and others were interred near Moreauville. (*This brick church was located in Hamburg on Bayou des Glaises, according to research by Steve Mayeux A descendant of the one of the soldiers buried came into the Weekly News office in 1990 with a letter describing the forgotten church. Mayeux determined the church site and cemetery mostly covered by the enlarged levee after the 1927 flood.)

Grismore said the Union buried their dead in the trenches on the Yellow Bayou. Some of those graves may have been later reinterred in the National Cemetery in Pineville in later years.

Lt. John Moncure wrote:
I was again with his regiment on Yellow Bayou and Bayou Gaize on the 18th, when it was led by the gallant Robertson, (Col. Terrell being yet un- well) and again I was with Terrell's Regiment, an advanced picket, when they escorted the last of the enemy across the bayou, and captured many horses and mules. (Transcribed by William J. Bozic, Jr. Dec 16, 2008.)

Crossing the Atchafalaya

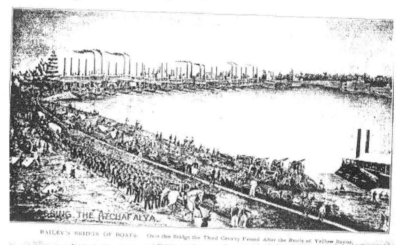

BAILEY'S BRIDGE OF BOATS. Over this Bridge the Third Cavalry Passed After the Battle of Yellow Bayou.

As the Confederates chased Bank's troops back to Simmesport, after the Battle of Yellow Bayou the Union Army found itself up against the Atchafalay which is at its highest in the Spring, and difficult to cross. So they improvised this bridge at Simmesport as sketched by John Needham Bellchamber of Co. C, 119th Illinois Infantry. It is one of several sketches in the possession of the Illinois State Historical Library, Springfield, Illinois.

Harris Beecher, a Union soldier of the 114th New York, wrote: *"Early on the morning of the 19th, the army commenced to cross the Atchafalaya, a portion, with all the train, moving over upon a bridge of steamboats, which was another product of the engineering skill of Lieutenant Colonel Bailey. The structure consisted of twenty transports, anchored abreast of each other, from bank to bank. Over their decks, timbers and planks completed a bridge of nearly fifteen hundred feet in length. About the middle of the forenoon, the One Hundred and Fourteenth was ferried over on the steamer Emerald . . . "*

Yellow Bayou and the 1st Vermont

by Edward E. Greenleaf, 1st Lt. 1st Vermont Battery, Light Artillery

At Yellow Bayou, Bayou de Glaise, and at the crossing of the Atchafalaya river the battery took a prominent part, also at above Alexandria, where the gunboats under Admiral Porter were detained at the rapids by low water, the battery was continuously on duty as guard during the building of the dam devised by Lieutenant-Colonel Bailey, to deepen the water in the channel and enable the gunboats to pass down the river.

At Yellow Bayou, May 18, 1864, two sections of the battery under command of Lieutenants Rice and Greenleaf were detailed to serve with General Mower's commands of the Sixteenth Army Corps, and formed part of the read guard of the expedition, during the remainder of the campaign, until after crossing the Atchafalaya river at Simmesport. The left section of the battery, under command of Lieutenant Greenleaf being the last troops to cross the river, the bridge which had been made by interlacing the bows of river steamers pointing alternately up and down stream, being broken up by withdrawing a steamer as soon as the battery had passed over it. After crossing, the battery returned to the original command and was highly commended by General Mower for the efficient service rendered.

Corp. A. McCurdy, Illinois Inf. KIA May 18

May 19, 1864
Report of U.S. Major General Nathaniel Banks:

The bridge was completed at 1 o'clock on the 19th of May. The wagon train passed in the afternoon, and the troops the next morning, in better spirit and condition, as able and eager to meet the enemy as at any period of the campaign. The command of General A. J. Smith, which covered the rear of the army during the construction of the bridge and the passage of the army, had a severe engagement with the enemy under Polignac on the afternoon of the 19th [18th], at Yellow Bayou, which lasted several hours. Our loss was about 150 in killed and wounded; that of the enemy much greater, besides many prisoners who were taken by our troops.

Maj. Gen. E. R. S. Canby arrived at Simsport on the 19th May, and the next day assumed command of the troops as a portion of the forces of the Military Division of the West Mississippi, to the command of which he had been assigned. Rumors were circulated freely throughout the camp at Alexandria that upon the evacuation of the town it would be burned. To prevent this destruction of property, part of which belonged to loyal citizens, General Grover, commanding the post, was instructed to organize a thorough police, and to provide for its occupation by an armed force until the army had marched for Simsport. The measures taken were sufficient to prevent a conflagration in the manner in which it had been anticipated, but on the morning of the evacuation, while the army was in full possession of the town, a fire broke out in a building on the levee, which had been occupied by refugees or soldiers, in such a manner as to make it impossible to prevent a general conflagration. I saw the fire when it was first discovered. The ammunition and ordnance transports and the depot of ammunition on the levee were within a few yards of the fire. The boats were floated into the river and the ammunition moved from the levee with all possible dispatch. The troops labored with alacrity and vigor to suppress the conflagration, but owing to a high wind and the combustible material of the buildings it was found impossible to limit its progress, and a considerable portion of the town was destroyed.

May 19th, 1864,
Report of U.S. General A. J. Smith

We reached the vicinity of Simmesport on the 16th, skirmishing with the pursuing cavalry. Our boats being there, a bridge was made of them across the Atchafalaya, and on the 17th, 18th, and 19th, the Thirteenth and Nineteenth Corps and the cavalry crossed the bayou.

Report of U.S. Major General Nathaniel Banks:

The 16th [?] of May we reached Simmesport, on the Atchafalaya. Being entirely destitute of any ordinary bridge material for the passage of this river (about 600 yards wide) a bridge was constructed of the steamers, under direction of Lieutenant-Colonel Bailey. This work was not of the same magnitude, but was as important to the army as the dam at Alexandria was to the navy. It had the merit of being an entirely novel construction, no bridge of such magnitude having been constructed of similar materials.

U. S. Major Gen. Nathaniel Banks   U. S. Gen. William B. Franklin

May 20, 1864
Report of U.S. General A. J. Smith

I crossed the bridge on the 20th, bringing up the rear, and marched to Red River Landing, on the Mississippi River, whither our boats had been sent, and reported, by order of Major-General Banks, to Maj. Gen. E. R. S. Canby for further orders, and was by him directed to proceed to Vicksburg with my command, which I did, reaching that place on the 23d of May, having been gone seventy-four days.

The results of the expedition may be summed up as follows: I captured with my command 22 pieces of artillery, 1,757 prisoners, and Fort De Russy, with a strong casemated battery, which the gunboats would not have been able to pass. My loss was 153 killed, 849 wounded, and 133 missing; total, 1,135; also 1 6-mule wagon. My entire command numbered originally 9,200.

Of the general officers attached to my command I cannot speak too highly. Brig. Gen. (now Maj. Gen.) J. A. Mower, by his perception and prompt action at Fort De Russy, Henderson's Hill, and Pleasant Hill, and by his gallantry and skill at Yellow Bayou, near Simsport, May 18, has won the right to a high estimate and position in the annals of the war. Quick perception, ready courage, an abundant vitality, added to skill and education, give him the power to sway men as if by magnetism. Brig. Gen. Thomas Kirby Smith, with excellent judgment and skill, brought the boats safely through the intricacies and shoals of Red River back to Grand Ecore, although continually under fire. His repulse of the cavalry charge upon his division at Cloutierville was well and neatly done. I commend him as a gallant officer and gentleman. I had hearty and energetic co-operation on the part of my brigade commanders, two of whom, Col. S. G. Hill, Thirty-fifth Iowa, and Col. William F. Lynch, Fifty-eighth Illinois, were severely wounded. Col. William T. Shaw, Fourteenth Iowa, commanding brigade, proved himself an excellent officer and rendered invaluable service at Fort De Russy, Pleasant Hill, and Yellow Bayou. He is a brave, energetic, and intelligent officer.

To all the officers and men of the command praise is due for their cheerful, enduring, and ready obedience. Each and all the officers of my staff were untiring and active in their respective duties. I am much indebted to their intelligent action and ready appreciation of the situation. Arms, eyes, and heads seemed their main attributes during the whole campaign. I add their names as a matter of record, as their well-deserved promotion has overtaken all who are now in service: Capt. John Hough, assistant adjutant-general; Capt. William S. Burns, Fourth Missouri Cavalry, acting assistant inspector-general; Capt. J. J. Lyon, Twenty-fourth Missouri Infantry, judge-advocate; Surg. N. R. Derby, medical director, wounded May 18; Maj. E. A. Warner, Fourteenth Iowa Infantry, provost-marshal; Capt. Ross Wilkinson, aide-de-camp; Capt. Samuel Caldwell, Eighth Illinois Infantry, acting aide-de-camp; Lieut. George W. Fetterman, Fifteenth U. S. Infantry, assistant commissary of musters; Lieut. John B. Pannes, Seventeenth New York Infantry, ordnance officer.

I have the honor to be, with much respect, your obedient servant,

A. J. SMITH, Major-General.

Steamer Switzerland on Red River

Whithall Plantation, built by B. B. Simmes, founder of Simmesport. The home was used by Gen. N. Banks. It still stands today.

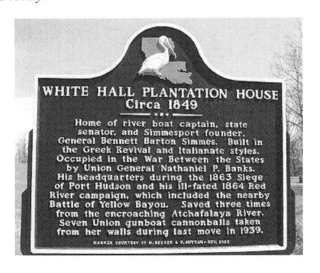

May 24, 1864 river cannons

Siege Batteries made up of heavy artillery were placed on the banks of the Atchafalaya River at Simmesport to prevent the passage of the gunboats.

May 24th, 1864 Simmesport gone

Silas Grismore left a sad description of what was left of Simmesport as the 18th Louisiana Infantry camped on Bayou des Glaises on May 24th: *Today the army of Gen. Banks finished crossing the Atchaflaya River at Simmesport. Our brigade was soon after removed near the spot upon which that little village stood, but the village was one of the things of the past.*

The men were able to salvage pieces of chain and gears from wagons and carriages which had been destroyed at Simmesport. The 18th remained at the camp in Simmesport for several days

May 24th, 1864 Confederate report

The report of CSA Cavalry Commander John Wharton who ordered and supervised the CSA forces at Norwood's Plantation/Yellow Bayou gives a different angle of the Battle of Yellow Bayou:

To The Officers and Soldiers
    Of Wharton's Cavalry Corps:
Army of West Louisiana, In The Field,

May 24th, 1864

Soldiers! For forty-six days you have engaged the enemy, always superior to you in numbers. When the beaten foe (four army corps of Infantry and five thousand cavalry) began his retreat, you were formed in battle array in his front, and being upon his flanks and rear, only to destroy. In his retreat from Grand Ecore to Atchafalaya, you killed wounded and captured four thousand men, destroying five transports and three gunboats. All this was accomplished with a loss to you of only four hundred men, two-thirds of whom will report for duty again within forty days. The history of no other campaign will present the spectacle of a cavalry force capturing and killing more of the enemy than their own number. This you have done, and, in so doing, you have immortalized yourselves and added new lustre to Texas--the gallantry of whose sons has been illustrated on every battlefield from Gettysburg to Glorietta. Had a portion of our forces been where I was informed they were, one hour and a half before the engagement at Norwood's Plantation, the rear guard of the enemy would have been entirely destroyed; as it was, thirty of his dead were left on the field, and sixty-five graves inscribed "killed in action on the 18th of May," besides his wounded carried away by him, testify to the slaughter you inflicted upon him. Federal prisoners, recently captured, announce their loss at eight hundred men, killed and wounded, at Norwood's Plantation. Your advanced guard are now watering their horses in the Mississippi River, wither you will soon follow. On short rations and with scanty forage, and in the saddle day and night, you have neither murmured nor complained.

In all your trials, the veteran 2^d Louisiana Cavalry have been by your side. They have shared your dangers, and are participants in your glory.

During the entire retreat, the different Batteries of Artillery, either acting separately or under command of Col. Brent or Maj. Simmes, displayed the most marked skill and gallantry. They were particularly distinguished in the engagement at Norwood's Plantation

I as commander honor you for your deeds, and thus acknowledge my appreciation of your services.

Gen. Taylor cheerfully accords to you the need of his approbation, and, in his own time and way, will signify his admiration.

A grateful people will cherish the record of your gallantry.

JOHN A WHARTON, Major General
Official Wm. I. Moore, A.A.A.G.

Transcribed on Dec 28, 2008 by William J. Bozic, Jr. from the *Houston Daily Telegraph*
All Rights Reserved.

May 26, 1864 Barbarous acts in Avoyelles

Besides the horrendous stories on the war front, two horrific events are recorded in Avoyelles during this time period. Some freed slaves who had been following the Yankees fell sick and then were abandoned in Simmesport. On May 26th, Poche wrote: *The negroes who had smallpox were left behind in Simmesport, and have been killed and burned by our pickets. On all those roads the air was impregnated with the tainted and intolerable odor of red horses and men.*

Around this time, former 18th soldier Leopold Siess of Mansura, and some of his followers of were captured, along with his half-brother, Isaac Lehmann, by a Confederate militia. The men had been sympathetic to the Union and were led in a "Home Guard: Captain Frederick Masters of Marksville, who headed a notorious band of Union sympathizers. Siess managed to escape through an open window, leaving Isaac and the others behind. The next day nine of the oldest men, including twenty-four year old Isaac were taken into the woods at Holmesville, in the southwestern corner of Avoyelles where they were stripped, and shot as traitors. Period newspaper accounts characterized this as one of the most barbarous acts of the war,.

Alphonse B. Coco Home, probably site of Camp Coco. (Carlos Mayeux Photo)

May 30th, 1864, Camp Coco hospital

The 18th had moved their camp for next couple of weeks, at Lake William, still near Simmesport. Felix Poche recorded in his diary on May 30th, that *This morning accompanied by Dr. McPhutur [McPheeters], surgeon of our Brigade, I rode in the ambulance, and went to Moreauville, to visit our wounded in Camp Coco. Those unfortunates suffer greatly from the heat, and are truly bothered by the flies and other insects. We returned to camp at 2 o'clock.* "Before sunset, Adjutant Blackman and I went horseback riding down the DesGlaizs, and returned at dusk."

Camp Coco probably may have been on the plantations of Alphonse Bienvenue Coco in Moreauville, whose plantation home stood facing Bayou des Glaises just north of the location of the Sacred Heart Cemetery. This plantation was the closest to the center of Moreauville and along the most traveled intersection of roads leading to Big Bend, Marksville, Evergreen and Simmesport.

It may also have been located on the nearby plantations of his brothers, Philogene outside of Moreauville on the LongBridge road or F. B. Coco on the Borodino Road.

June 8, 1864
Final skirmish of the Red River Campaign

The final action in the Red River campaign was on June 8, 1864 in Simmesport during an artillery battle with the Union Army.

Felix Poche recorded in his diary of this action on the Atchafalyaa:

Wednesday June 8.

Early this morning we heard heavy cannonading in the direction of Simmesport, and we learned the cause about noon. Three of the enemy's ironclad gun-boats came and attacked two of our pieces at Simmesport, and after a terrible cannonade, one of our pieces exploded and the other was put out of action. The Crescent Regiment which was on picket was immediately placed in a position to prevent the enemy from disembarking. At that point the enemy's fire was so severe that the Crescent was obliged to take refuge back of the Des Glaizes levee. The only way to save the pieces was for the regiment to charge across the field, but Capt Claiborne knowing that it would cost him many men decided not to risk any more lives, knowing that the cannon was not worth fifty or sixty men, who would inevitably be killed." The Yankees had one or two men disembark who tied a rope around the cannon, pulled it aboard the boat, and left rejoicing in their good fortune." The loss was of no consequence but the incident will be given such an undue importance in the eyes of the Yankees that I bitterly regret that little disaster.

Section II

Portraits of Confederates in uniform who served during the Red River Campaign

Portraits marked with this Cross:

is a designation of "died in line of duty"

Col. Leopold L. Armant,

Killed at the Battle of Mansfield

Arthur Pendleton Bagby, Jr.
Led his brigade from Mansfield to Simnmesport
(May 17, 1833 – February 21, 1921) Texas lawyer, editor

Bagby's cavalry brigade was renowned as one of the best in the Trans-Mississippi Department He led his brigade the Battle of Mansfield during the Red River Campaign. Bagby's cavalry then harassed the retreat of the Union Army under Major General Nathaniel P. Banks from Mansfield to Simmesport, Louisiana. General E. Kirby Smith assigned Bagby to duty as a brigadier general on April 13, 1864, to rank from March 17, 1864. Bagby commanded a brigade under Brigadier General Hamilton P. Bee for a time before replacing Bee in command in mid-May 1864.

Col. James Hamilton Beard, of Desoto Parish

Commander of Consolidated Crescent

Killed at the Battle of Mansfield

Brig. Gen. Hamilton Prioleau Bee
(1822-1897)
Field Commander, Red River Campaign
Texas Congressman, veteran of Mexican War.

Brig. Gen. Hamilton Bee was a field commander under Lt. Gen. Richard Taylor in the Red River Campaign. In the Battle of Pleasant Hill, Bee had two different horses shot out from under him during a cavalry charge, but was only slightly wounded.

Capt. Alonzo B. Boren, *Co. "K" 35th (Likens) TX Cavalry Regiment, CSA*

(1830 Macon GA- 1902 Gilmer, Texas)

Capt. A. B. Boren was on duty with Likens' Regt in the Indianola and Powderhorn, Calhoun County, Texas March 19 1864 when the order came to move to stop the Union advance up the Red River. He rode with his regiment arriving in time for the April 8, 1864 Battle of Mansfield. His letter to the Tyler Reporter newspaper, published April 12th, vividly described his disdain for the behavior of the Union troops towards the innocent people of Louisiana.

A request was written by Boren to the AAG requesting a leave of 60 days due to poor health from being in the field fighting for months without end, the effects of which have left him unfit for duty. Approved by Capt Gus E. Warren of Co. "G", who was temporarily commanding the regiment, October 5, 1864 while in camp near Evergreen, La. Capt Boren returned to Texas and in November 1864 he married Sallie Elizabeth Johnson.

Source: William Bozic

Major David French Boyd,
Builder of Fort DeRussy, 2nd President of LSU

Boyd, an engineer, was captured near Fort DeRussy by some "jayhawkers" who brought him to Natchez and sold him to Federal Troops for one hundred dollars. Fortunately, his teaching comrade, now Union General W. T. Sherman was nearby. Boyd was escorted by guards into a room with Sherman and the two men were very happy to see each other. "How do you do Professor Boyd! I am glad to see you, very glad indeed. Sherman was able to keep Boyd from going to a prison camp and arranged for him to be exchanged for Union soldiers captured in the Battle of Mansfield.

Augustus Buchel
Col., 1st Texas Cavalry

Killed April 9 at Pleasant Hill

At the outbreak of the Civil War Buchel joined the Texas militia; late in 1861 he was made lieutenant colonel of the Third Texas Infantry and served in South Texas. He became colonel of the First Texas Cavalry in 1863 and saw extensive service on the Texas Gulf Coast but was transferred to Louisiana when the threat of an invasion of Texas by Union troops became imminent. He was mortally wounded while leading his troops in a dismounted charge at Pleasant Hill, Louisiana, on April 9, 1864. He was taken to Mansfield, where he died and was buried. The generally accepted date of his death is April 15, but Gen. Hamilton P. Bee, Buchel's commander, related in his official report of the battle that he died two days following the battle, on April 11.

James P Byrne 1829-1864
2nd Sgt. 28th Louisiana Grays, Co. C.

Killed at Pleasant Hill, April 9, 1864

Leo Pierre Champagne,
Pvt., Co. D, 18th LA INF

Rolls from July, 1863, to Feb., 1864, Present. On Hospl. Register, Admitted Oct. 15th, 1864, to C. S. A. Gen. Hospl., Shreveport, La

Confederate 1st Lieutenant W. B. Champlin,(1836-1920)
William Belden Champlin
Lt., 2nd Louisiana Cavalry
Champlin, William B., 1st Lt. Co. D. and F. 2nd La. Cav. En. June 30th, 1862, Iberville, La. Roll for Jan. and Feb., 1863, Absent. Sick. Federal Rolls of Prisoners of War, Captured near Salt Works, Nov. 30th, 1863. Sent from New Orleans, La., to New Iberia, La., Dec. 21st, 1863, \and exchanged. 2nd Louisiana Cavalry participated in Red River Campaign during battles at Henderson Hill and Mansfield.
Born in Stonington, CT, married in Natchitoches, LA, in 1868

Thomas James Churchill
13th Governor of Arkansas
Planter

Churchill served in the District of Arkansas of the Trans-Mississippi Department and commanded a division during the Red River Campaign. He played a major role in the Battle of Jenkins Ferry and was promoted to major general on March 17, 1865.

Private Pleasonton Grey Conner,
*Captured at Fort DeRussy at beginning of Red River Campaign
Died in Union Prison
Co. H, 19th Texas Inf.,
Walker's Texas Division, CSA*

Captain James M. Daniel,
Captain of Daniel's Texas Battery at Battle of Mansfield.

Brig. Gen. Xavier Blanchard Debray
1816-1895   Texas

Xavier Blanchard Debray (January 25, 1816 – January 6, 1895) was a French-born soldier and diplomat who immigrated to the United States, settling in Texas. During the American Civil War Debray raised a Confederate cavalry regiment from Bexar County and was appointed brigadier general before the war's end.

Lt.. Joseph Rafael De La Garza
of San Antonio, Texas

Killed at the Battle of Mansfield

Lieut. Oscar Augustus Durrum
3rd Texas Cavalry; 1st Texas Partisan Rangers
Mortally wounded at Mansfield April 9, 1864.
Enlisted at Jefferson, Texas, june 1861.
 Birth: 1840 Tipton County, Tennessee
Death: 1864, Mansfield, De Soto Parish. Louisiana

Capt. William Fuller of Natchitoches Parish

Company F, Consolidated Crescent

Killed at the Battle of Mansfield

Capt. Henry Garland
Co. B, 18th Infantry

Henry Gray

Brig. Gen. Henry Gray (1816-1892) was the original commander of the 28th (Gray's) Louisiana Infantry Regiment and commanded the Louisiana Brigade in the Red River Campaign of 1864.

Brig. Gen. Thomas Green ✝

Killed during Red River Campaign

(1814 – 1864) lawyer, politician, soldier, officer of Texas.

Green led his division of cavalry from Texas in the battles of Mansfield and Pleasant Hill. A few days later, on April 12, 1864, he was mortally wounded by a shell from a Federal gunboat while leading an attack on gunboats patrolling the Red River at Blair's Landing. U.S. Admiral David Porter paid tribute to Green saying that he was *"one in whom the rebels place more confidence than anyone else. He led his men to the very edge of the bank, they shouting and yelling like madmen —losing Gen. Green has paralyzed them; he was worth 5,000 men to them."*

Col. James M. Hawes, (1824–1889)
Commander, 1st Brigade of Walker's Texas Division

Hawes spent the winter of 1863-64 in camp near Marksville. On February 11, 1864, Hawes was relieved of command of the brigade at his own request and ordered to report to Gen. John Bankhead Magruder.

Capt. James G. Hayes
Co. K, 18th LA Inf

Col. Alfred Hobby, 8th Texas Inf.
In Bee and Waul Brigades

William M. Hogsett
19th Texas Infantry
1835-1913 Hopkins County, Texas

The 19th fought at the Battle of Milliken's Bend, Louisiana, on June 7, 1863, then, in 1864, participated in stopping the advance of Union General Nathaniel Banks up the Red River and pursuing General Frederick Steele's Union force from Camden to Little Rock. Company K was then detached to Marshall, Texas, for guard duty.

Colonel Richard B. Hubbard
22nd Texas Infantry

Captain John Kelso
Company B, 2nd Louisiana Infantry

Judge, Senator
1830-1870 of Rapides Parish

John Kelso was the original commanding officer at Fort DeRussy on Red River in Avoyelles Parish. A. J. Chambers Collection: Capt. Kelso's Co. A, Battt'n Hy arty La - March 22, 1863, Fort De Russey"" Vouchers and letters, including one dated May 1, 1863 for stationary "for myself as Commander of the Gun Boat Fleet," documents indicate he was Commanding Post at Alexandria, he is recorded as Assistant Inspector General, Office General Court Martial, Alexandria - SOURCE: Steve Mayeux:

Wilburn Hill King

KING, WILBURN HILL (1839-1910). Wilburn Hill King, Confederate officer, Texas state legislator, and adjutant general

He took command of Polignac's Brigade, Mouton's Division, when General Polignac departed to France. King was later transferred back to Walker's Division,

Claiborne Lane
Co. G, 18th Louisiana

Claiborne Lane, Co. G, 18th Louisiana is one of these two soldiers

Alexander A. Lesueur (1842-)
Captain, Tilden's Missouri Battery, CSA

In April 1864, Lesueur's Battery participated in the Red River campaign, then on to Arkansas to pursue Gen. Frederick Steele's Union army in his retreat from Camden; After the war, Lesueur settled in Lexington, Missouri, where he edited a newspaper and served in the legislature; in 1888 he was elected secretary of state,. He died in Burbank, California.

James Patrick Major (1836-1877)
Lieutenant, U. S. Cavalry then
Brig Gen., Confederate States Army

Planter in Texas and Louisiana.

Thomas Madison McNeely,
4th Sergt., Co. C, 18th Louisiana
Natchitoches

Dandridge McRae
28th Arkansas
Reserve brigade in Battle of Pleasant Hill

Pvt. Justillen Molaison
Co, G, 18th Louisiana

Image courtesy of Michael D. Jones.

Gen. Alfred Mouton of Lafayette
Killed at the Battle of Mansfield †

Thomas H. Murray (1835-1884)
*Lt. Col., 4th Missouri Infantry
Injured at Battle of Pleasant Hill*

Pvt. Christopher Columbus Nicad
Company C, Consolidated Crescent

Mosby Monroe Parsons
(1822-1865)
Virginia/Missouri
Brig. General, CSA
Assisted in thwarting advance of Union Gen. Bank's Army in Red River Campaign

Capt. Elijah Parsons Petty 1828-64

Killed during the Battle of Pleasant Hill in Louisiana, Sabine Parish. He was buried at his request under an oak tree, "so his family could find his grave". He was born in Dover, TN, son of John and Theora Bruton Petty, He married Margaret Elizabeth Pinner on January 3, 1849 in Stewart Co., Tennessee. They had five children.

Srgt. F. Numa Poche,
18th Louisiana Infantry

Captain Simeon Alexandre Poche, (1831-1912)
Co. B, 18th Louisiana Infantry
(Dave Poche Collection)

Prince de Polignac
(1832-1913)
French nobleman promoted to General for his leadership at Mansfield

French resident took over command of 19th Louisiana Infantry
when Gen. Mouton Fell at Mansfield.
Last living Confederate general when he died at age 81 in Paris

Jacques Alphonse Prudhomme
(son of Pierre Phanor Prudhomme and Suzanne Lise Metoyer) was born 17 Apr 1838 in Oakland Plantation/ Natchitoches Parish, LA, and died 17 Feb 1919 in Oakland Plantation, Natchitoches

18th Louisiana Infantry

Participated in Battle of Mansfield

Gen. Horace Randal
Commander, 28th Texas Cavalry
Killed May, 1864

Some members of the 28th Texas Cavalry were at Fort DeRussy when it fell in March of 1864. Later, at the Battle of Mansfield, April 8, 1864, during the Red River Campaign, Randal's brigade broke the Union line and took about 500 prisoners and the Union Army wagon train while leading the pursuit of the fleeing Federal force. On April 13, 1864, General E. Kirby Smith appointed Randal to duty as a brigadier general. Randal and his brigade also performed with distinction at the Battle of Pleasant Hill on April 9, 1864. Randal was mortally wounded while leading a charge at the Battle of Jenkins' Ferry, the culmination of the Union Camden Expedition under Major General Frederick Steele, which was part of Major General Nathaniel P. Banks's larger Red River Campaign, on April 30, 1864. He died on May 2, 1864 and initially was buried near the battlefield.

Thomas Richard Rice 1842-1887,
DeWitt County, Texas

Sergeant in 2nd Texas Cavalry Regiment, 2nd Mounted Rifles,
Engagement, Wilson's Farm, Apr 7, 1864;
near Pleasant Hill LA, April 8 & 9th 1864;
Skirmish, Bayou de Paul (Carroll's Mills) April 8, 1864
Battle, Sabine Cross Roads, April 8, 1864;
Mansfield April 8, 1864;
Skirmish, Cloutiersville, LA, April 23 - 24, 1864;
Skirmish, Alexandria, LA, April 27 - 29, 1864; May 13, 1864; Skirmish, David's Ferry LA, May 3, 1864;
Action, Graham's Plantation, LA, May 5, 1864;
Skirmish, Bayou LaMourie, LA, May 6, 1864;
Operations against the Retreat from Alexandria to Morganza, LA, May 13 - 20, 1864;
Engagement, Yellow Bayou, Bayou de Glaze Norwood

Plantation (Old Oaks) LA, May 18, 1864;

R. W. Sanders,
Co. D, 1st Lt., 18th LA Inf.

Leonce Sandoz
St. Martin Rangers, The Bull Battery
Opelousas Courrier Newspaper publisher

In the spring of 1864 he was one of the little garrison of Fort DeRussy, composed of a part of his company and some of Bird's command, about thirty men. Being attacked by Gen. A. J. Smith's 10,000 man Federal division, they were captured March 14th, after two hours' hard resistance, in which about forty of the enemy were killed or wounded.. Sandoz and Dr. N. D. Young, of Rayville, escaped by a subterranean passage, but were recaptured next day, and sent to New Orleans, where they were held as prisoners until the following August, exchanged at Morganza Ferry. Subsequently Sandoz was on outpost duty in St. Martin's parish then Grand Ecore, until the surrender.

William Forrest Sinclair
1826-1895 of Desoto Parish

William Sinclair, of DeSoto Parish, was a member of the Texas group, Terrell's Cavalry Regiment [also called 34th and 37th Regiments]. The unit was assigned to H. Bee's and Bagby's Brigade, Trans-Mississippi Department, and fought in various locations in Louisiana.

The unit saw action at Mansfield, participated in the operations against the Federal Red River Campaign, and was active at Lecompte and Yellow Bayou. In May, 1865, the regiment disbanded at Hempstead, Texas.

Brig. Gen. William Read Scurry
(1821 – 1864)
Commanded Walker's 3rd Brigade at Mansfield

Scurry was born in Gallatin, Tennessee. He moved to Texas in 1839 and became a lawyer and district attorney.
 Appointed brigadier general on September 12, 1862, he along with fellow New Mexico Campaign veterans, he helped recapture Galveston, Texas on January 1, 1863.
Scurry then took command of the Third Brigade of Walker's Texas Division in October 1863 and led them into the Battle of Mansfield and Pleasant Hill, April 1864.

Gen. Edmund Kirby Smith, CSA

Edmund Kirby Smith (May 16, 1824 – March 28, 1893) was a general in the Confederate States Army, notable for his command of the Trans-Mississippi Department of the Confederacy after Vicksburg fell.

Brig. Gen. James Camp Tappan
(1825 – 1906)
Led brigade at Pleasant Hill

Graduate of Yale Law School
Arkkansas attorney

Tappan commanded his brigade at the Battle of Pleasant Hill in Louisiana, defending against Maj. Gen. Nathaniel Banks' Red River Campaign of 1864. After the fight at Pleasant Hill, Tappan's brigade was moved northward back into Arkansas to meet General Frederick Steele at the Battle of Jenkins' Ferry.

Lt. Gen. Dick Taylor

Commander of First Louisiana Brigade, CSA
Commanded Army of Western Louisiana in the
Red River Campaign

Son of President Zachary Taylor

Cpl. Paul Thibodaux
Company G, 18th Louisiana Infantry
Courtesy of Stan Hutson
Wounded at Shiloh on April 7th
Lafourche Parish

Pvt. C. L. Van Houton, Co. C, 18th Louisiana
*Image from Portraits of Conflict of Louisiana, by Carl Moneyhon &
Bobby Roberts*

Leonce Sandoz
16th Battalion aka St. Martin Rangers
Publisher of Opelousas Courrier Newspaper

Maj. John Vernon,
Hobby's Regiment, The 8th Texas Confederate

Capt. Richard Stanley Venables
Adjt. Capt. Co D, Crescent Regt.
Native of New York
Resident of New Orleans

SERVICE RECORD: Venables, Richard S., Adjt. Capt. Co. D, Cres. Regt. La. Inf. En. New Orleans, La., March 5, 1862. Roll May and June, 1862, Present, promoted from 2nd Lt. to Capt., May 22, _. Rolls from Nov., 1862, to Aug., 1863, Present. Federal Rolls of Prisoners of War, Captured Pleasant Hill, April 9, 1864. Delivered by Maj. Gen. Banks, U. S. A., to Maj. Gen. Taylor, C. S. A., April 20, 1864, at Blair's Landing, La. On Official Rolls of Paroled Officers, C. S. A., Paroled Natchitoches, La., June 6, 1865.

John George Walker (1821 – 1893) was a Confederate general. He served as a brigadier under Jackson and Longstreet, before commanding a Texan division in the Trans-Mississippi Department, known as Walker's Greyhounds for their speed and agility. He was ordered to disrupt Grant's supply-line opposite Vicksburg, but Grant had managed to cross to the East bank, and Walker was reduced to minor operations, one of them against some of the first African-American troops to serve in battle. He was able to make a bigger contribution to the Red River campaign, in support of General Dick Taylor.

Harvey Wallace
19th Texas, Captured at Fort DeRussy

Lt. Col. Edwin Waller, Jr.
13th Texas Cavalry
The 13th battalion participated in the Red River Campaign from Fort DeRussy to the battles of Mansfield and Pleasant Hill, Moreauville and Mansura

Thomas Neville Waul (1813-1903)

Brig. Gen. Thomas Neville Waul
Replaced Hawes in Marksville in February, 1864
Captured at the fall of Vicksburg on July 4, 1863. Promoted to brigadier general September 18, 1863. His performance and leadership were commended by General Stephen D. Lee. Waul then commanded a brigade in John Walker's division in the Confederate Trans-Mississippi. Waul's brigade fought in the Red River campaign. He led the brigade from Marksville to Mansfield.

Section III

Confederate Order of Battle

Red River Campaign

Confederate Order of Battle during the Red River Campaign

Operations in Louisiana, March–May 1864

The Orders of Battle was documented by Civil War expert and author Gary Dillard Joiner.

Dr Joiner is the director of Red River Regional Studies Center, Louisiana State University in Shreveport, and also serves as president of the Friends of the Mansfield Battlefield.

Confederate Forces

Gen. K. Smith   Gen. R. Taylor

General Edmund Kirby Smith
 commanding the Army of the Trans-Mississippi
Maj. Gen. Richard Taylor
 commanding the District of Western Louisiana
Headquarters Escort Company (Louisiana Cavalry)—Capt. Joseph Benjamin
Unattached—2nd Battalion Louisiana Reserves

First Infantry Division

Mag Gen Walker
Commander, First Infantry Division at Mansfield

Gen. Waul   Col. Young   Col. King   Col.Hubbard Col. Crawford

First Brigade—Brig. Gen. Thomas N. Waul
12th Texas Infantry—Col. Overton C. Young
18th Texas Infantry—Col. Wilburn H. King
22nd Texas Infantry—Col. Richard B. Hubbard
13th Texas Cavalry, Dismounted—Col. Anderson F. Crawford
Haldeman's Texas Battery—Capt. Horace Haldeman

Col. Randal   Col. Roberts   Col. Clark

Baxter   Gould   Capt. Daniel

<u>Second Brigade—Col. Horace Randal</u> (<u>promoted brigadier general April 13</u>)
11th Texas Infantry—Col. Oran M. Roberts (Later Governor)
14th Texas Infantry—Col. Edward Clark
28th Texas Cavalry, Dismounted—Lt. Col. Eli H. Baxter Jr.
6th (Gould's) Texas Cavalry Battalion—Lt. Col. Robert S. Gould
Daniel's Texas Battery—Capt. James M. Daniel

Lt. Col. Scurry   Col. Flournay   Col. Allen   Col. Waterhouse

Fitzhugh   Capt. Edgar

Third Brigade—Brig. Gen. William R. Scurry
3rd Texas Infantry—Col. Phillip N. Luckett (attached about April 15)
16th Texas Infantry—Col. George Flournoy
17th Texas Infantry—Col. Robert T. P. Allen
19th Texas Infantry—Col. Richard Waterhouse Jr.
16th Texas Cavalry, Dismounted—Col. William Fitzhugh
Edgar's Texas Battery—Capt. William Edgar

First Division Artillery
Haldeman's Texas Battery—Capt. Horace Haldeman
Gibson's Battery
Daniel's Texas Battery—Capt. James Daniel (Also in 2nd brig)
Edgar's Texas Battery—Capt. William Edgar (Also 3rd brigade)

Mouton   *Polignac*   *Beard*   *Gray*

James Hamilton Beard, Desoto Parish
Killed at Battle of Mansfield
28th LA INF

Second Infantry Division
Brig. Gen. Jean Jacque Alexandre A. Mouton (killed April 8), Brig. Gen. Camille Armand Jules Marie, Prince de Polignac

First Brigade—Col. Henry Gray
18th Louisiana Consolidated Infantry—Col. Leopold L. Armant (killed April 8), Lt. Col. Joseph Collins (promoted colonel)
28th Louisiana Infantry—Lt. Col. William Walker (killed April 8), Maj. Thomas W. Pool (promoted colonel)
Consolidated Crescent Regiment—(Louisiana) Regiment—Col. James Beard (killed April 8), Col. Abel W. Bosworth, Capt. William C. C. Claiborne, Jr.

Second Brigade—Brig. Gen. Camille J. Polignac, Col. James R. Taylor (killed April 8), Lt. Col. Robert D. Stone (killed April 8), Co. James E. Harrison
15th Texas Infantry—Lt. Col. James E. Harrison (promoted colonel April 15), Maj. John W. Daniel (promoted lieutenant colonel April 15)
17th Texas Consolidated Cavalry, Dismounted—Col. James R. Taylor, Maj. Thomas F. Tucker
22nd Texas Cavalry, Dismounted—Lt. Col. Robert D. Stone, Maj. George W. Merrick
31st Texas Cavalry, Dismounted—Maj. Frederick J. Malone

34th Texas Cavalry, Dismounted—Lt. Col. John H. Caudle

Lt. Bennett   *Capt. Benton*   *Gen Churchill*   *Gen. Tappan*

Artillery—Maj. Thomas A. Faeries
Confederate Regular Battery, Capt. John T. M. Barnes
Bell (La.) Battery—Capt. Thomas O. Benton
Boone's Louisiana Battery (siege guns)—Lt. Maunsel Bennett
St. Mary (La.) Cannoneers—Capt. Florian O. Cornay (killed April 26), Lt. John B. Tarleton.
Second Division Artillery—Maj. Joseph L. Brent (promoted lieutenant colonel)
Reserve Battalion—Maj. Charles W. Squires
West's Arkansas Battery—Capt. Henry C. West
Pelican (La.) Battery—Capt. B. Felix Winchester

Detachment, District of Arkansas
Brig. Gen. Thomas James Churchill

First Division
Brig. Gen. James C. Tappan
Tappan's Brigade—Col. H. L. Grinstead
19th (Dawson's) and 24th Arkansas Infantry—Lt. Col. William R. Hardy
27th and 38th Arkansas Infantry—Col. R G. Shaver
33rd Arkansas Infantry—Col. Hiram L. Grinstead
Etter's Arkansas Battery—Capt. Chambers B. Etter
Gause's Brigade—Col. Lucien C. Gause
26th Arkansas Infantry—Lt. Col. Iverson L. Brooks
32nd Arkansas Infantry—Lt. Col. William Hicks
36th Arkansas Infantry—Col. James M. Davie
[? 39th Arkansas Infantry—Col. James W. Rogan?]

Marshall's Arkansas Battery—Capt. John G. Marshall

Capt. LESUER   Gen. PARSONS

Second Division
Brig. Gen. Mosby M. Parsons

First Brigade—Brig. Gen. John B. Clark Jr.
8th Missouri Infantry—Col. Charles S. Mitchell
9th Missouri Infantry—Col. Richard H. Musser
Ruffner's Missouri Battery—Capt. Samuel T. Ruffner
2nd Brigade—Col. Simon P. Burns
10th Missouri Infantry—Col. William M. Moore
11th Missouri Infantry—Lt. Col. Thomas H. Murray
12th Missouri Infantry—Col. Willis M. Ponder
16th Missouri Infantry—Lt. Col. Pleasant W. H. Cumming
9th Missouri Battalion Sharpshooters—Maj. Lebbeus A. Pindall
Lesueur's Missouri Battery—Capt. Alex A. Lesueur

Cavalry Corps---------------------------------------
Brig. Gen. Thomas Jefferson Green (killed April 12), Brig. Gen. Hamilton P. Bee, Maj. Gen. John A. Wharton

Gen. Bee   Xavier Debray   Gen. Wharton   Col Buchel

First Division
Brig. Gen. Hamilton P. Bee (relieved May 14),
Brig. Gen. Arthur P. Bagby
Debray's Brigade—Col. Xavier B. Debray (promoted Brig Gen.)
23rd Texas Cavalry—Col. Nicholas Gould (arrived April 9–10)
26th Texas Cavalry—Lt. Col. John J. Meyers
36th Texas Cavalry—Col. Peter C. Woods (arrived April 9–10)
Buchel's Brigade—Col. Augustus C. Buchel (mortally wounded April 9), Col. Arthur P. Bagby   (promoted brigadier general April 13), Col. Alexander W. Terrell
1st Texas Cavalry—Lt. Col. William O. Yager
35th (Likens') Texas Cavalry—Col. James B. Likens, Lt. Col. James R. Burns (arrived April 9–   10, detached to Sub-District of North Louisiana)
Terrell's Texas Cavalry—Col. Alexander W. Terrell

Gen. Major   Col. W. Lane   Col. Bagby   Col. Baylor

First Division
Brig. Gen. James P. Major
Lane's Brigade
—Col. Walter P. Lane (wounded April 8),
  Col. George W. Baylor
1st Texas Partisan Rangers
—Lt. Col. R. P. Crump, Maj. W. P. Saufley
2nd Texas Partisan Rangers
—Col. Isham Chisum, Lt. Col. Crill Miller
2nd Regt., Arizona Brigade

—Col. George W. Baylor, Lt. Col. John W. Mullen
3rd Regt., Arizona Brigade
—Lt. Col. George T. Madison
Bagby's Brigade
—Col. Arthur P. Bagby, Col. William P. Hardeman, Lt. Col. George J. Hampton, Lt. Col. Edward Waller Jr.
4th Texas Cavalry—Col. William P. Hardeman, Lt. Col. George J. Hampton, Maj. Charles Lesueur
5th Texas Cavalry—Maj. Hugh A. McPhaill
7th Texas Cavalry—Lt. Col. Philemon T. Herbert Jr. (promoted colonel; mortally wounded April 8), Lt. Col. Gustave Hoffman
13th Texas Cavalry Battalion—Lt. Col. Edward Waller Jr., Capt. W. A. McDade
Vincent's Brigade—Col. William G. Vincent (independent)
2nd Louisiana Cavalry—Col. William G. Vincent, Maj. Winter O. Breazeale
4th (7th) Louisiana Cavalry—Col. Louis Bush
Horse Artillery—Maj. Oliver J. Semmes
Grosse Tete (La.) Flying Artillery Battery—Capt. John A. West
Gibson's TX Battery—Capt. William Gibson (arrived c. May 10)
McMahan's Texas Artillery Battery—Capt. Martin Van Buren McMahan
Moseley's Texas Artillery Battery—Capt. William G. Moseley
Valverde (Tex.) Artillery Battery—Capt. Thomas D. Nettles
Louisiana State Guard
1st Louisiana Battalion Cavalry—Lt. Col. Benjamin W. Clark, Maj. Thomas J. Caldwell
2nd Louisiana Battalion Cavalry—Lt. Col. Henry M. Favrot

T. H. Hutton

Miscellaneous

Harrison's LA Cavalry Battalion—Lt. Col. William Harrison
Red River Scouts (La.) Cavalry Battalion (two companies)—Capt. Willis A. Stewart
1st Trans-Mississippi Cavalry Battalion—Maj. Thomason J. Bird
King's Louisiana Battery (siege guns)—Capt. Edward T. King
Crescent Artillery (Company A)—Capt. T. H. Hutton

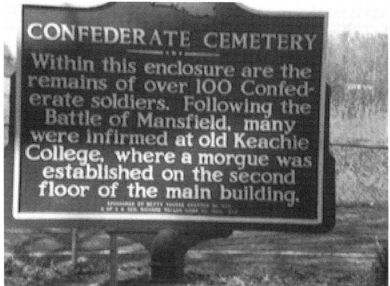

Confederate Cemetery at Keatchie